Shift & Drift

The Galway Player's Guide to Dating in Ireland

The world of Irish dating through
the eyes of its greatest player …

BLACKWATER PRESS

ISBN 978-1-909974-03-6

BWP Ltd., 1-5 North Frederick Street, Dublin 1
Printed in the Republic of Ireland.
jloconnor@eircom.net

"This book would not have been possible without the support of my amazing family, a great bunch of friends and a certain lady who inspired me more than she'll ever realise ...".

Contents

What's Love Got to Do with It?

Picture the opening scene of *Saving Private Ryan*. Now add fake tan and copious amount of vodka and red bull. Welcome to your average Saturday night out in Ireland. To the uneducated outsider, the mating rituals of Irish youths look as sophisticated and thought out as the Irish Health System. Yet this is Plan A for finding your soul mate, the person that you want to raise the fruit of your loins. The one that you'll promise to be true to in good times and in bad, in sickness and in health, love and honour for all the days of your life. A shift, a Supermacs and, if you're serious about her, a friend request on Facebook.

Dating is constantly evolving. Like mobile phones, it's hard to keep track of the developments. Past generations didn't have to deal with relationship status, tagged photos, check-ins and the countless other perils of modern technology. That's where I come in. Like Richard Attenborough, I have dedicated my adult life to watching, observing and interacting with the countless fascinating creatures that you come across.

Many of you will know me, but my identity is irrelevant. I have spent countless nights out honing my skills in the clubs, pubs and fast food joints of our fair city. I am the Lionel Messi of dating, I score for fun and have brought the game to a new level, I may not be the greatest ever, but I'm definitely in the top one! Watch all the romantic comedies you want, read all the magazines on the shelves, but if you want to know the truth about dating in Ireland, I'm here to tell it like it is.

I see lads make so many basic mistakes every weekend, stupid things that if they had a mentor could be the difference between waking up beside a half eaten burger or a smoking hot babe. As a cantankerous Cork man once said, "Fail to prepare, prepare to fail", and for once he was right. Like a team preparing set pieces, tactics and formations before a game, guys need pre-match rituals too. From what you wear, to the stories you tell, what you're drinking, to sealing the deal – I'm your man! For definitive advice that actually works, this book is essential reading.

Don't worry ladies I'm not forgetting you, not only will you get a unique insight into a unique male mind, I will also be dispensing advice to the fairer sex. I will be covering topics like fake tan (currently a bigger crisis in this country than the national debt), what to wear, what his texts really mean, how to attract the right kind of guy and how to keep him happy. Ladies, think Gerard Butler in *The Ugly Truth* and you're on the right track to the kind of legend you're dealing with – but unless you're a Katherine Heigl lookalike – jog on.

Educating the Nation

We're a curious nation. My research (sleeping with non-Irish girls, mainly American students but it still counts) indicates that dating in Ireland is undoubtedly unique, not without its charms, yet undeniably flawed. Why are we such a funny little island? Could it have anything to do with our education system?

Our first foray into the big bad world generally begins in September of our fifth year on this intriguing planet. The typical Irish classroom is a fascinating place and plays a central role in shaping us as people. The mental scars caused in these very impressionable years, can certainly be cited as some of the contributing factors to the countless flawed adults we encounter all too often. Put simply, if you bake a cake with the wrong ingredients how do you expect it to turn out okay?

You can't analyse the education system in this country without first looking at the foot soldiers – the teachers. Truly, one of the most fascinating species around. Leaving my own personal experiences of dating teachers aside, they annually divide the nation *à lá* Roy Keane 2002. It's easy to castigate them for all the holidays and short hours they work, so that's exactly what I'm going to do. Yes there's lesson plans and extra curricular activities, which, let's be honest, are rare. But at the end of the day it's for kids. If you can't spoof a few 8-year-olds, then education probably isn't the career for you.

Through extensive research – chatting up teachers in bars – I have a number of radical suggestions that will revolutionise the Irish education system.

How are kids going to grow up as well adjusted adults if their role models are the likes of Justin Bieber, Jedward, Miley Cyrus and soccer players? A scan of tweets by fans of the aforementioned are insightful and frightening, so we need role models that kids can identify with and learn from; the majority of the current crop of teachers are well wide of the mark here.

We can't have the future minds of this planet being moulded by the current occupants of the country's classrooms. With all due respect, teachers are:

Lazy

Most only go for the profession based on the holidays. Honestly who can blame them? It sure beats working for a living.

Bitter

Not initially, but after years of repeating the same mundane lessons to group after group of cheeky brats. Kids are grand for an hour or two, your own for a bit longer, but dealing with other people's offspring for a living, it's enough to drive you nuts.

Unromantic

Anecdotal evidence suggests that over 90% of teachers marry other teachers or Guards. It's not exactly *The Notebook* is it? "Where did you meet Miss?" "St Pat's".

Immature

Again, simply a side effect of the job, but sometimes when you're having a discussion with a teacher, you have to remind them that you're not a 7-year-old kid in the classroom, and giving you extra homework isn't how you resolve an argument.

My idea, which I will be sending to the relevant authorities once this masterpiece is completed, would be that teachers can only serve in the role for a maximum of seven years – much like the President. I really don't understand how it takes the current crop three years to study *Busy at Maths* and *Ann and Barry*, so we'll do a three-month training camp for my new recruits during the summer and they can hit the ground running in September. We need to hire interesting people, who can inspire our future leaders and emigrants. A massive stumbling block seems to be the need for Honours Irish, the simple solution here is to hire Hector O'hEochagáin and Sile Seoige to record a Rosetta Stone type video series which the new breed of cool teachers could just press play and the focus on other important things to teach the kids.

I'd insist that the male teachers play sport, a proper one too – nothing daft like orienteering or running. It's an ideal job for a GAA head obviously, but rugby has the respect element of not talking back to referees, which wouldn't go astray in any classroom. Soccer players make great Geography teachers. I was years ahead of my peers when it came to capitals based on a passion for international soccer.

The ladies should be stylish, we could recruit from the vast pool of SoSueMe wannabes, the thousands of female fashion bloggers could impart their knowledge on impressionable minds. Ireland would be a much better place if young girls were buying Caudalie Eye & Lip Serum, Stila Lip & Cheek Pallets and Catrice Ultimate Lash Mascara instead of naggins of vodka and cans of Dutch Gold. Also these teachers should be in good shape. We constantly hear about childhood obesity – fit teachers would find it a lot easier to inspire their classes.

Hazrat Ali told his son, Imam Hasan: "The child's mind is like the virgin land. Whatever is put into it, will be accepted. Therefore, before your heart turned hard and engrossed otherwise, I took steps to make you polite."

I don't have any idea who these people are, but I thought a quote from a foreign-sounding person would add to my argument, plus he's basically reiterating what I've just said. By the time they get to secondary school, teenagers are much harder to mould in a positive way. Primary school is the key and until my strategy is implemented, well-rounded young people like me, will continue to be the exception rather than the rule.

Looking back now it's like another lifetime, the innocence of our nation's school days was something we never fully appreciated. The only drink problem we ever encountered was spilling the carton of warm milk in our oversized school bags after lunch. Unless you were in a mixed school, the only bit of eye candy you got to awaken those as yet unexplainable feelings, was during English lessons, when that little pig-tailed minx, Ann flirted her way through the pages of our lessons, and into the hearts of many a young man. Even at that age I was ahead of my peers, let's just say I liked the way the mother was put together – even then.

Mixed schools were obviously the way forward, allowing balanced integration from an early age, plus games of spin the bottle when you got to the big classes. Nowadays, kids probably use an app for these games, but in our innocence, it got you more excited than the TV and VCR being rolled out.

Con-Fidence

That's the political rant over, now to the real reason you're reading this book – to learn from the master. Let's start at the beginning, the corner stone of being successful with the opposite sex is self-confidence. As an expert on the female psyche, I use the knowledge that I have amassed during my days on the Galway social scene to great effect. It's not just that I know the names of all the bouncers in town.

Self-confidence is one of the most critical attributes any man can possess. It trumps looks, wealth and sense of humour, but in reality, is the foundation for all of these. Like a great team with a terrible back four in soccer, you're asking for trouble if you don't focus on getting this right first.

Self-confidence, real or contrived, can open so many doors in your life, particularly doors to bird's bedrooms. Fake it till you make it; is the mantra of many successful people. We all know bluffers whose success defies logic. Many friends of mine now hold responsible jobs, the kind of lads that make Dan Bilzerian look like a boring accountant. Genuine talent doesn't always lead to confidence, it's all about attitude. Of the many gems in my arsenal, one of the best tricks I find is to tell birds that I'm not interested in them as I already have a girlfriend. Since women, all women, are bitches, this is actually one of the best things you can say to help you score. It takes a lot of confidence to reject someone you desire ... but it works!

Think about it lads, how many times have you gone ages without any female attention and as soon as you start seeing someone, it's like a Lynx ad, quality birds throwing themselves at you? Go out this weekend with a coupled up friend and take a note of who gets the most female attention. Why is this I hear you ask? Well, I believe it dates back to our earliest ancestors. In prehistoric times, women picked a partner based purely on his physical presence, ability to gather food and provide shelter. Now it's much more difficult, weak men can be rich and good providers. Your average cave woman probably wouldn't go for Bill Gates now would she? Now women find it much harder to identify prospective partners, I blame *Sex and the City* and a whole host of romcoms for setting unrealistic hopes for women.

"All the good men are taken" is the battle cry of many single women up and down the country, while their vaginas cobweb over, but in truth, the men that are taken are only perceived as good. In a recent study in the University of Oklahoma, single women favoured men with partners significantly over their single counterparts. I believe that in women's eyes, value is confirmed by the company of other women. Basically a goofy looking guy hanging out with an absolute babe will have all the other tea makers wondering exactly what this guy has going for him. I've often toyed with the idea of experimenting with a 'wing woman' but never did, I feel their morals and emotions would interfere with the scoring process. Women seem to think that a guy with a partner means that he is good enough for someone else, so he may be good enough for you. Also he's not afraid of commitment and he's a sap that will do what he's told.

The trick is to know how to use this information to your benefit. Women are attracted to confident men, and if you have a girlfriend you are not trying too hard, you have no fear of failure, therefore you are confident. In addition, the naturally jealous nature of women will make you irresistible. Remove the fear of failure and you can achieve anything. But how do you do that if you're single?

Self-confidence or the Inner Game as the great Pick Up Artists call it, can be controlled and improved by you yourself. I always preach the importance of looking well. Leaving the house looking the best you can is something you choose to do. Sadly too few in society accept this challenge. Until there's an actual fashion police society, we will continue to crumble. Each time a girl wears her pyjamas down to the shop a fashion blogger dies a little on the inside.

Remember the speech in *Any Given Sunday* that Al Pacino gave to the Miami Shakes? It still sends a shiver down my spine, proof that words can inspire. As my chat-up lines inspire women to sleep with me, so you can inspire yourself to be more confident. I know that standing in front a mirror telling yourself "I am the man" can make you feel like a bigger tool than a JCB but if you don't believe it, how will anybody else? I've worked this into my daily morning routine, despite the fact that I regularly get distracted and lose track of time staring at my own reflection. I know it sounds strange to refer to a man as beautiful, but who am I to go against popular opinion?

I can imagine some of you saying it's easy for me to talk about self-confidence, for far too many young men in particular, see it as a foreign concept. Everyone has bad days, when nothing seems to be going right, or ever will. Perspective is paramount, try to be objective, I'm not saying that you shouldn't be upset about getting dumped, losing your job, etc. but there's always someone worse off than you. This is like telling a bloke after witnessing a particularly devastating defeat to cheer up because "it's just a game".

What I recommend is to build it up slowly. Like trying to get out of a dry spell with birds, when you end up scoring a five just to get back in the saddle. Small achievements will set you on the road to success, working out, eating healthy for a full week, getting a few matches on Tinder.

The mind is an incredible tool, and if you truly believe in yourself and stay positive, it's not the only incredible tool that you'll be exercising regularly. When it comes to dating it's just a game!

Bromance

As a proud Galwegian, I often find myself drowning my sorrows after local sporting disappointments. Along with my companions, we hit the local to drown our sorrows in the bottom of a pint glass. We start off as miserable as a delinquent who can't find his favourite shoes to wear with his good tracksuit for his trip to court, but after a few hours of shooting the breeze about sports, birds and slagging the shite out of each other, all is good in the world once more. It's at times like this that your mates really come through for you.

In fact, one of the many great things about being a man, apart from the world being your toilet, is having a Bromance. A Bromance is a heterosexual male's feeling of platonic love for another man that is reciprocated by his bro. Some of the most famous bromances include Ben Affleck and Matt Damon, Turk and JD (culminating in the song *Guy Love*, the good kind) Joey and Chandler. Great male friendships have even inspired a number of great movies including *Wedding Crashers*, *I Love You Man*, *Butch Cassidy & The Sundance Kid*, to name but a few.

Hanging out with your bro means that you can do stuff that you actually enjoy with someone you care about. You can go to matches together, spot each other in gym, head out on the pull together, play FIFA 15 and discuss the important issues in life – like which condoms help you last the longest, which bar has the hottest women in town and doesn't mind lying to a bird to big you up and get you your hole.

Of course girlfriends have their uses, but in terms of looking at the bigger picture, apart from blowing your load, a bro has countless advantages over a bird.

A lad will never say it was only a game when your team lets you down worse than the flesh cannon going off too early. He understands that every game is a matter of life and death and every game is the most important game ever, until the next one.

Lads are never out of commission for one week in the month and moodier than the poor bastard who got Lisa Reilly in *Strictly Come Dancing*. If a guy is in a bad mood, you can actually ask him what's wrong and get a straight answer. Trying to get a straight answer out of a woman would be a challenge for Jeremy Paxman.

I always prefer to watch a flick with the lads, women don't appreciate my insights in the same way. The last bird I had over apparently didn't share my interest in giving Reese Witherspoon a one way ticket to pleasure town.

Basically women aren't as much craic as lads. My now famous version of *Snog, Marry or Avoid*: *Shag or Don't Shag* never receives the same howls of approval from birds that it does from the lads.

The difference between male and female friendship is that the male version is real, it's based on common interests which mean something. Women have friends so they have a platform to meet a husband and someone to bitch about the fact that there are no nice guys left, even though in reality the nice guys turn them off faster than the thought of a night of passion with Brian Cowen after a skip of porter and a dirty kebab.

One of the Lads

Any sports fan will recognise that while everyone aims for the same result, there are countless ways of achieving this: all out attack, counter attack, a defensive approach, depending on set pieces, etc. There are days when you know you're unbeatable and other times you wonder how the hell you pulled that result out of the fire. The uncertainty of it all is what makes sports, just like dating, so interesting. A recent night out gave me an opportunity to observe approaches to scoring as diverse as the approaches of Dublin and Donegal to the beautiful game.

Here are a few of the different characters that I observed:

The Pretty Boy

Ridiculously good looking and knows it. All he has to do is stand there looking good, and let the ladies form an orderly queue. The problem is that when they do approach, he is about as interesting as reading the iTunes terms and conditions. He's like the tallest lad in the parish when you were playing underage football; he never had to jump to catch high balls in games, so when everyone else grew up, he lacked the experience and technique to perform at the highest level.

The Caveman

In from the sticks for the night, grunting and farting his way through the night, this guy is generally as charming and likeable as an STI. He is very persistent, like a door-to-door sales man who you just can't get rid of and before you know it you're sponsoring a village in North Leitrim. The Caveman will corner his prey and wear her down; the smell of Clonmel champagne from his breath will overpower the hum of Lynx Africa.

The Mammy's Boy

He's very polite and nice, looks like his mother just dressed him, shirt tucked in to his y-fronts. He's a slow drinker because he's checking out all potential targets around the room – that he's lacking the confidence to approach. He spends so much time in the Friendzone, that the last time he saw a girl naked he was applying fake tan to her back as he slowly died on the inside. Women, like wolves, can smell the fear and insecurity and this lad has as much hope of scoring as Liverpool do of winning a trophy before the next 12/12/12.

Doesn't Try At All

On a night out, there is only one thing that excites this lad and creates any kind of stirring in his loins – and that is a good pint of Guinness. This lad is only out for the craic and could be getting a lap dance from the best looking bird in the place, but all he is concerned about is his next drink. It's not that he's completely against the fairer sex and once the last drink is served, he makes lumbering and often misguided attempts at courtship which could see him wake up anywhere or with anything from a traffic cone to Susan Boyle's ugly sister.

The "I Would Have"

He's got a night off, planning permission was sought weeks in advance and free from she who must be obeyed, he is that man. He's like Clarke Kent without a phone box in sight. Every bird that walks by, apparently wants him or is eye-fucking him from across the bar. The modelesque blonde knocking away guys like Rafa Nadal returning second serves, could be his, if only he was single. He's loving the position of being the man, he's secretly texting herself every five minutes, promising that he's behaving and claiming that he'd prefer to be at home with her watch Ryan Tubridy drooling over Katherine Jenkins on *The Late Late Show*.

I suppose they can't all be legendry lotharios like my good self ...

Bird Watching

Like a hurling replay, no two nights out are the same. The build up, the anticipation, the hustle and bustle of it all, and then the in-depth analysis. It's a break from the constant grind of the working week. For some, a good night out involves waking up face down in a box of taco cheese fries, but for the likes of myself, success is measured by the quality of the companion you wake up beside. As a keen student of Irish nightlife, I have observed and encountered an impressive array of categories of women. Like David Attenborough, I have spent countless hours watching, interacting with and documenting intriguing creatures.

Any given Friday or Saturday night out can see you bump into the likes of:

Super Macs

This girl looks like she has just walked away from the Mac counter in Brown Thomas. Her make up is flawless all night, requiring countless trips to the bathroom to touch herself up, decreasing her hopes of getting touched up herself. She's the kind of bird that'll ruin your sheets, but she'll most likely have disappeared before you stir in the morning, for fear she'll be seen without the war paint. High maintenance but great to be seen with early in the night, not one for PDAs in case you smudge the plaster.

Ghost Estate

These girls are lovely looking, ideal for a single guy, comes with all mod cons, seemingly perfect girlfriend material, yet they remain alone and uninhabited. Nobody has entered the premises in quite some time. You wonder why these girls are single, until you try to chat them up. During her own boom period things went awry, and she's never fully recovered. She'll drink most lads under the table and would challenge Diversity with her efforts on the dance floor. Harder to bring home than Sam Maguire for the Mayo team, a big fan of the Sunday session and Clonmel champagne.

The iPhone 15

This lady has the lads queuing up for her all night. She's a thing of beauty and seems to have a spell over men. She loves to tease lads, she'll lead them on, let them buy her drink and then moves on to her next victim. Like Samantha in *Sex and the City*, she's a man eater, very confident in her own sexuality and knows how to play the game. She's the Premiership and the average guys are fighting relegation. You'd need to be super wealthy or as good around the box as Van Persie to get her.

The Wedding Planner

Unfortunately it's not because she's a Jennifer Lopez lookalike, it's due to her desperate search for a husband. This girl cuts straight to the chase and before you've downed the first pint, she's sizing up how you'll look in the wedding photos, if you'll get a decent mortgage between the two of you, and whether your genes will produce good offspring. The loudly ticking biological clock and smell of wedding cake are always a clue, but watch out for the ring finger which will be throbbing when she encounters a viable potential wedding facilitator, by that I mean – a man.

Avensis

She's safe, sensible, comes with plenty of attractive features and won't let you down. Popular with guards and other civil servants, this lady is pleasing on the eye – especially when new and if you service her regularly, will do you for years, until you trade her in for a newer model. The kind of girl you can bring home to Mammy and the lads will like her too. Generally a big soap fan and can be found mentally wrestling between a Saturday night out with the girls or staying in to watch X Factor with a bottle of Pinot and enough rice cakes to safely package a 42" Plasma TV.

The Jäger Bomb

It seemed like a great idea last night, it's ten to two – she'll do. Rough as a bear's arse, but in the smoking area of the dimly lit nightclub, she looked like Mila Kunis' better looking sister. The little head was thinking for the big head, the repercussions are just something you have to suffer through, and hope it goes away soon after waking up. You'll swear to the lads you'll never do it again, until the next time you're out with the beer goggles on.

The Yummy Mummy

Single mothers are incredible women to be fair, I can barely look after myself and they have the wherewithal to live a fully functioning life and raise a few rugrats. These women deserve to be shown a good time in their rare free moments, so when the opportunity arises I'm more than happy to oblige. There's no bullshit with these ladies and after spending the majority of their time with kids, they are extremely appreciative of some adult company. As long as she's not looking for a father for little Johnny, single mothers are A1.

You Are What You Wear

Men are visual creatures, we can't fight this – it's in our DNA. Show a guy a photo of a nice side boob and he's revved up faster than a Lamborghini Huracán. While women also appreciate an attractive member of the opposite sex, they don't have the same primitive urges as men. Accepting this fact ladies, you must excuse men's sometimes less than subtle appreciation of your form. The site of an attractive well-dressed woman is what gets me up in the morning. We know that when you wear that low cut top you're getting them out for yourself, it's a given. A lingering glance is no more that a pat on the back, saying "Good job, I'm a big fan of your work".

However, an all too common and distressing sight which nobody needs or wants to see, is something that's etched into my memory. I recall a rather large lady in my direct eye line wearing what was basically a backless top, this individual had more rolls than a bakery. Now this is not an affront on overweight people, it is more friendly fashion advice. Quite frankly, the more this girl covered up the better for all concerned. My biggest problem is how her friends let her out in this fashion faux-pas. We all know that sometimes you have to be cruel to be kind, especially when it's in the person's and society in general's best interest, then it has to be done.

Apart from friends, I am calling on the staff of Ireland's favourite fashion outlets. Of course it's great to get a sale, but you need to look at the bigger picture – or bigger customer in this case and say no, when you see a blimp waddling towards the counter with a top that would barely cover her arm never mind the rest of her. You need to stop and think are you actually helping anyone through this transaction? Some birds are like the atrocious singers on *X Factor* whose deluded performances make for amusing TV and help the rest of us feel much better about ourselves. How many times have you asked yourself "Who told that tone deaf muppet they could sing?" Well bring that mentality on a night out and have a good look around.

Obviously addressing those in society who are, shall we say, easier to see, is frowned upon because they are seen as an easy target. Regardless, there is a problem and I for one, am not afraid to shine a light on this massive issue. I'm no SoSueMe, but dressing well is essential. Regardless of your shape, size or budget you can find clothes which will make you look and feel more attractive. You don't need a personal shopper following you around to know that if you have more spare tyres than Advance Pitstop you don't wear a dress that looks like you were poured into it.

Here's another quick tip ladies, want to get rid of muffin tops? Try wearing jeans that fit! Something else to avoid is short shorts, last weekend I observed a bird with more cellulite than you'd see at an ICA meeting. Hot pants are only for hot birds, hence the name. Unless you're after some sort of chubby chaser – cover up!

Men's fashion has definitely come under the spotlight in recent times also. More and more Irish guys now know the difference between Louis van Gaal and Louis Vuitton. Sadly, it's still impossible to flick through the photos of any rural Irish nightclub or bar on a Monday and not see at least one lad wearing a check shirt in each photo. Most of these albums end up being like some kind of magic eye photo.

Realistically, there is no excuse for guys dressing badly, there's so many decent clothes shops locally that you can pick up bargains in. It's not all about labels these days thankfully, but that doesn't mean that men shouldn't invest in a few staples that will pay for themselves over time. Shoes, a suit, a good coat – which can double as a funeral coat – very important in the sticks, and a decent haircut, are areas that I wouldn't skimp on.

A passion for fashion is no longer the preserve of women, gay men and hipsters (a trend which will fortunately only survive one generation due to the oppressively tight skinny jeans causing infertility – insufferable twats). My own sartorial elegance is both revered and appreciated amongst my peers. Birds, booze, football and fashion are now the common topics discussed by lads on a night out. I say discussed, I obviously mean a merciless character annihilation if one of the group fails to hit the mark, fashion wise.

A GAA dressing room is a fascinating melting pot of fashion clichés. Your average team will contain most or all of the following fashion victims/victors:

Gym Bunny

Tight is Right – as long as the guns are on display the outfit works for this gent.

Sensible Seáns

They wear O'Neill's tracksuits and the club T-shirt to the game and the Wranglers and check shirt out after. Like in the game, no fancy stuff – it's all about getting the job done.

College Boyos

The young lads have a winter in DCU under their belts and return home with skinny jeans and T-shirts buttoned up to the top, much to the disgust of the local contingent.

Flash Johnny

Every team has at least one eccentric with the all year round tan, normally the free taker, he was the first one in the parish to wear white boots, he's living in the big city and always uses the dinner dance to preview next season's trends.

The beauty of fashion is that you don't need to live in Milan, Paris or New York to keep up-to-date. Thanks to social media, in particular Instagram, you can follow some ridiculously cool fashionistas while you're in Mullingar, Portlaoise or Newtownmountkennedy. I'd still advise that you bring a stylish bird with you when you go shopping or at least Snapchat a few selfies before you buy.

Society has set the standards for beauty and I am urging people to follow them. As Oscar Wilde once said, "One should either be a work of art, or wear a work of art." If you don't have it (or you've got too much of it) then please don't flaunt it.

You Are What You Drink

You Are What You Eat was a TV show where an annoying woman used to dissect shit to tell fat people they were eating too much. I believe that your drink tells a great deal about you, however I merely rely on my observation skills and a few chats with Galway's best barmen to compile a list which has been of great benefit to myself and the lads on our quest for love.* The pub scene is fascinating at the best of times, I've often thought of jacking in the day job to become a barman, they really enjoy a unique insight into human behaviour, particularly in the cooler pubs around town.

So lads here is a list of a few popular drinks and what they mean:

Vodka & A Dash

I'm always happy to see a bird holding one of these. This lady is drinking to get merry, like most Irish women has no actual

*we love one night stands

knowledge of drink and most probably can't taste the vodka after drowning it in Coke or TK lemonade. She's generally hot and very self-conscious, drinking vodka to keep the weight down.

Pints

Seriously dude avoid this one like the plague. In my book it's only acceptable for tourists who will sit looking at it all night. Pints are for men end of story. Any ladette swamping pints with the guys clearly doesn't care about her weight, appearance or ever actually meeting anybody of the opposite sex.

Alcopop

If she's necking one of these she's young, doesn't like the taste of alcohol yet, very likely to be on her knees at the end of the night, but it's 50/50 whether it'll be puking up what looks like radioactive vomit or giving you head.

Double Vodka & Red Bull

An interesting character here, watch out for these birds, they are crazy and liable to do anything, out for a good time, will be well on, but the Red Bull will ensure she'll have lots of energy for nocturnal activities, most likely filthy in the bedroom. It's not a cheap round, so wait until the end of the night to chat her up.

Wine

Very popular in older women like 30+. They are trying to appear classy and sophisticated, but wine is generally just a leg opener. Women try to appear choosy when selecting wine, they generally know very little about it and nine times out of 10, Pinot Grigio is what the birds drink, it'll make you look good when you make the selection for her.

Gin & Tonic

Favoured by mature and refined ladies, be careful – these birds are generally high maintenance and could finish the night balling her eyes out at the end of your bed. Sadly Sile Seoige's drink of choice, otherwise we could have been the Posh & Becks of Galway.

Cosmopolitans

She thinks she's in *Sex and the City*, you're not Carrie – darling – you may look like a farmyard animal in the morning but that's as close as you get. It's drink to get drunk, normally on a girl's night out, so I see cocktails as a one way ticket to bang town.

While I'm on the subject, ladies here's what his drink tells you:

Guinness/Stout

He's a farmer – probably that bit older, and will stink your bedroom out the next morning. Buying rounds on a busy night is annoying because you have to wait for the old man's drink to settle.

Lager

One of the lads, a proper man – and this guy is boyfriend material. Bring him home tonight.

Bottle

He's not a big drinker, it's a risky one. The saving grace is that he's probably a safe bet for later.

Paulaner/ Hoegaarden / Budvar

Any of these foreign beers or Micro Brewery jobs. He's pretensious, a hipster, will bore you to tears about his knowledge of European beers and *über* cool music that nobody listens to. Then he'll hate it as soon as it becomes commercially popular – avoid!

Vodka

He's Eastern European or a gay Irish man – whatever you're into I guess. Sports players have begun to drink this during the season, it's not a bad line but could end up getting more numbers from lads than ladies.

Bulmers

He's a farmer. If you're a country girl go for it, ye will have little farmer babies and live on a farm, doing farm stuff.

Wine

If he's not drinking it with dinner and you're female, it's unlikely you're his type.

Fosters/Bavaria

He's either a student or really cheap, actually he's really cheap either way. He'll claim that it tastes okay, it doesn't – he's tight and unless you generally use a high heel to open your bottle of wine, keep going.

Lucozade

He's just in to watch a match and will be gone within one minute of the final whistle. Big into sports, probably spends his Saturday nights in watching *Match of the Day* and polishing his boots, he can remember how many goals Messi has scored with his left foot form between 25-35 yards out on a Wednesday, but struggles with what you've just told him.

Bar A Miracle

To say the Irish like a drink is like saying Kim Kardashian takes the odd selfie. Life in Ireland basically revolves around alcohol, from christenings to funerals and everything in between, the local boozer is the focal point of activity. If Ireland was a Simpsons character we'd be Barney Gumble. A quiet night out for most Irish people is enough to consign other nationalities to rehab. A friend of mine once announced that he was 'off the beer' for November, seeing our dumbfounded faces, he quickly reassured us that it was just beer – he'd still be drinking spirits.

I'm not condoning or berating the culture I'm just telling it like it is. Most workers begin work on a Monday morning counting down the hours till they can head out on the following Friday. The weather is often described using references to alcohol, 'it's beer garden weather' or 'it's a day for a hot one', directions are given almost exclusively using pubs as references. I know lads that approach a day on the beer with more determination or conviction than I've ever seen them display at work or on the pitch. A hangover is like a badge of pride in this country, proof that you gave it everything the previous night. When asked "How was last night?" the anticipated response is simply "dying".

Given this background, it's unfortunate that the primary location to meet someone is still the pub. Online dating has made leaps and bounds in recent years but the vast majority still depend on the local for love. I'm not a big drinker, my eye is always on the prize and beer goggles and a misfiring mickey are occupational hazards for a player like myself. Stumbling, sweaty, incoherent apes grinding up against a clearly uncomfortable victim is commonplace in pubs the length and breadth of our funny little country. Most guys can't see signs from women at the best of times, but stone drunk as most of them are before they consider an approach, she could be holding the John 3:17 sign from GAA matches and they'd still miss it. Women often have no choice but to get drunk enough to think these lads are actually charming. I can only imagine the amount of awkward conversations the morning after that being with "so how did we start chatting last night?" or worse still, "what's your name again?" It's pretty difficult to recover from that, but many do in all fairness.

The question has to be asked – is chewing the face off someone in a dark bar or club after consuming enough alcohol to sustain a country pub for the week, the best way to meet someone? Since we spend the vast majority of our time at work it would be ideal to meet someone there, but this has too many potential drawbacks. Never shit on your own doorstep or shag in the staff toilets is a lesson to live life by. Due to the acrimonious nature of break ups, its not worth the risk of a few months of fun followed by the nuisance of looking at your ex's miserable scowl creating tension at work until she finally builds a bridge.

I see the world as a place that has three types of women, the women I have slept with, the ones I haven't slept with yet and the one's that I'd never sleep with. I see every social interaction as an opportunity to get a number, why limit yourself to the pub on a Saturday night? Getting petrol, ordering food, a visit to the hospital have all proved successful in the past and no doubt will again. The element of surprise actually always works in my favour, as most women aren't used to being asked out by someone who's sober. Always have a pen and paper on you, it makes you look important; don't have the number written out already because that will make you look sleazy. Ask for her number so that you're in control of the situation.

Every time you meet someone is a chance for a conversation, on an island of talkers this is pretty easy. People in the service industry are often going through the motions at work, so a random amusing interaction will surprise and engage them. You're not going to ask out every bird you chat to, but the conversation skill will certainly stand to you when you are confronted by someone you are attracted to. No point in meeting the best looking bird in the place and going quieter than Thomond Park for a conversion. Public transport, not that I use it myself, is ideal for striking up conversations. Instead of having your head buried in your mobile for the journey, try to chat to the bird beside you if she's decent. Mates of mine used have massive success on the Sunday night journey west for college, four hours on a Feda bus from Letterkenny to Galway is enough time to start a relationship.

Admittedly, heading out at the weekend is the shop window for most of us, it's the opportunity to let the hair down, get all dolled up, throw on the glad rags and hit the town and I'm sure birds feel the same too! Still as a social drinker and a keen anthropological student, the pub scene frustrates me no end. We need a change in mentality, I feel like Eamon Dumphy criticising Jack Charlton's Irish team in 1990, but while it might be achieving results, we have the skill and people to achieve it in a far more aesthetically pleasing and enjoyable way. A more thorough, structured approach could be the real key to sustained success, but at the moment the masses are happy with lobbing long hopeful balls in the general area of the box and hoping that the odd effort hits the target.

Morning after the Night Before

W e've all been there, woken up with a mouth as dry as an Arab's sandal – your head feels like it's been used as the match ball in an Ulster Championship match. You're trying to piece together the previous night and a stirring in your bed alerts you to a guest. You breathe deeply, trying to recall the name of your latest conquest and you silently pray that in the harsh cold light of day, she's as smoking hot as you thought she was last night in that dimly lit bar that you met, talked and ate the face off her in.

Hopefully sufficient recollection has returned in order to engage the young lady that your charms so clearly had the desired effect on last night. A sneaky peak is called for to ensure that you haven't ended up bedding Free Willie or an Oompua Loompa, that is unless she's already awake. The big question is do you want/are you up for some morning fun? It's a bit like the cold Papa John's pizza from last night, if it's still there why not get stuck in? A few bathroom essentials are key before you instigate round two. Mouthwash is a must, while you can brush you teeth and fix the mop make sure she is aware of the Listerine, morning breath is a real turn off. Other essentials to have in your bedroom include a clean football jersey for her to sleep in, and you to pull off, non-scented moisturiser – they always ask for it, trust me. Birds also look for a hairbrush but it'd just be weird to have one, so forget about that. If you're playing away from home you just have to make the best of what's available to you.

Conversation can be awkward to say the least Of course it was no problem last night as you downed enough Jägerbombs to sink your average St Patrick's Day float. This is actually an area in which I excel, I always find humour is the only way to go, it puts the bird at ease and after you did all the hard work last night why not enjoy yourself?

Playful teasing and an offer to make her a cup of tea will guarantee you more action than any Galway footballer will see in Croke Park in September – if only it was that easy the night before. Once you've had your fun and as you're telling her how wonderful she is, all the while making sure you're using language evasive enough not to commit to anything you'll regret later.

Generally a one night stand is just that, you only wanted one thing and since you got it, now it's time to move on. Most guys are at a loss as to how to get rid of this unwelcome guest. Being well prepared can sort this out quickly, for example, before I head out the night before, I throw a full gear bag at the end of my bed, so when I tell her that I need to go for a match or training, it looks realistic. Telling her that your parents are calling over is a great tester. Store your own number as Mum and text yourself, "On the way over, do you need anything from the shop?" If that doesn't send her running out the door faster that a fat kid when they hear the ice-cream van outside, then you're in trouble. A sly text to one of the lads to call you for a fake pick up, is also an option. I've told more that one bird that I need to get up because my girlfriend is calling over, you might get a slap from the slapper but it gets the job done.

If all else fails and this should be easy enough after a night on the beer, you can use some dirty tactics and stink her out of it, but deny all ownership just to mess with her head. One piece of advice lads, always ring the taxi for her and be a gentleman and throw her a tenner for the fare so that she knows you're a nice guy.

Having your bedroom thoughtfully laid out can solve so many problems, as I will explain in the next chapter, the thing to remember here is that we all enjoy one night stands, just be safe and have an exit strategy planned.

The Magic Room

In the dating game, as in life, it is very difficult to be in complete control of any situation, unless it comes to the awarding of penalties to away teams at Old Trafford. One area you can control is your own bedroom, use it to frame you in the most positive light possible. This is where all the magic happens in my apartment – and I'm not talking about doing card tricks. Some of this is common sense and parts of it are ideas that I have picked up over the years.

It goes without saying that your room should be clean and tidy before you head out – the bed made, no jocks or socks left lying on the floor, maybe a jumper or shirt lying on the bed for effect, you don't want to seem too good to be true. Common sense would dictate that you either don't have or just hide your massive laminated Georgia Salpa poster before you entertain. I actually have a framed poem on my wall, the Robert Frost classic *The Road not Taken* it shows birds that I'm a thinker:

> *Somewhere ages and ages hence,*
> *Two roads diverged in a wood and I,*
> *I took the one less travelled by*
> *And that has made all the difference.*

Deep eh?

Photos give a bedroom character, any bird's room I've ever been in – and that is a significant number, you see lots of pics all over the place. I have a fair selection, if it's a one night stand, then I have pictures of me and a few hot birds left around the place, it makes her work that bit harder for my affections. If it's a date that I have over, then I hide those photos and put out a couple of pictures of me and the family, and I have printed out a picture of some kids in Africa, and I have a great sad story about building a church in Mali, it works every time.

Other ways of imposing your personality on the room include having a set of golf clubs in the corner, basically it's a classy sport and it shows that you like to head off with the lads to play a round, or around! I have a selection of trophies on my dresser, everyone has crappy looking medals – what I have displayed are all Galway Crystal or Player of the Year type things. I am lucky to be a very talented sportsman, if you lack my skills it's very easy to buy the trophies yourself and the inscription can say whatever you want. The same dresser proudly holds a number of books covering a very specific range of topics, travel, fine food, cocktails, sports; it shows my wide range of interests and intellect. I also have a book called *How To Do Just About Everything* which I always hilariously joke that I wrote.

I have an iPod dock beside the bed to play a few tunes to help improve the mood, nothing worse than waking up ready to go again and listening to some morning Jock – like a verbal contraception killing the mood. Yankee candles are a serious knickers dropper; they are a no brainer for a present for chicks too. Lighting is crucial, a couple of bedside lamps help here, you control the lighting so that you see what you want. If she's a babe get a sexy striptease before she joins you in the sack if she's more Gail Platt than Gail Kim then the darkness is probably her friend.

One of the legends of the game, Johnny Deep used to have a six foot rooster in his bedroom and he'd ask girls if they wanted to come back to his place to see his massive cock – brilliant! I'm debating getting a teddy bear, women love them and you can make up some sob story about the bird that broke your heart, or that some granny gave it to you after you saved her cat by getting him down from a tree, etc.

The morning after, when you are having a shower or making her a cup of tea, she will be looking around the room to figure out what kind of guy you are. My room paints a picture of what a great guy I am, ensuring that I am set up for another round if I want it. If I'm not up for seeing her again, when I see her out, I normally spin the bimbo around a few times so she forgets which apartment she just came out of.

Youth is Wasted on the Young

"Youth is wasted on the young", they tell us, I for one agree. Of late, I have been keeping company with a delightful 18-year-old babe and I am fully appreciating the joys of youth. The levels of energy and enthusiasm that they bring to the table are invigorating, not to mention the fact that they'll believe almost anything you tell them – makes dating younger women a very attractive proposition.

In reality, age is only a number, when it comes to ages gaps in relationships it's an issue of mind over matter. If you don't mind, it doesn't matter. Much more important factors are things like background, personality, sexual chemistry and how hot she is. When it comes to dating, I believe if she's hot enough – she's old enough. I'm not a bouncer, it's not up to me to ask for ID, so if she's in the bar and she deserves a shot at the title then who am I to argue? This nonsense of half your age plus seven is just wrong, think about it, you're a fit healthy outgoing guy who is say 50, ladies under 32 are off limits – that's just wrong.

Don't get me wrong I don't go out just to meet young girls, but it's important to understand some of the benefits of dating younger women:

✓ She isn't stressing about settling down or having kids (coz she's practically one herself).

✓ She's very easy to impress, younger women haven't been on the social scene that long, so haven't heard all my lines already.

✓ In the bedroom what she lacks in experience, she makes up for in enthusiasm and energy.

✓ The ravages of time have not yet taken their toll so she's still firm, tight and perky.

✓ Possibly most important, young women today are absolutely filthy, if I didn't enjoy the benefits of their sexual liberation so much, frankly I'd be disgusted at the antics I've been subjected to.

The yardstick by which most women seem to judge all of life's big questions, is to base it on the – oh so sensible – celebrity world, for once I don't mind! The younger woman thing seems to be quite popular among the rich and famous. Harrison Ford is married to Calista Flockhart who is 22 years his junior. Bruce Willis is nailing a bird 23 years younger than him. Catherine Zeta Jones is a quarter of a century younger than Michael Douglas. Another living legend Rod Steward is with the smoking hot Penny Lancaster who is 27 years younger than the Scottish rocker. We all know about the comic genius Woody Allen and his relationship with the young Sonn-Yi Previn, but what's 34 years when you're in love?

A quick Google search will enlighten us as the variations in the age of consent, ranging from the frankly perverse Spanish and Japanese who set the bar at 13 which is just daft, the US and UK set the limit at 16 and in Cameroon is a ridiculous 21, seriously what kind of crazy country is this? Probably not as bad as the likes of Saudi Arabia, Qatar, Oman, Bolivia and Bahrain where you need to be married to have sex ... ROFL.

I have nothing against the older ladies, in fact, I know that they have a lot to offer, particularly in the bedroom, however, dating a younger woman is something every man should try once, like not wearing jocks for a whole day at work, it's liberating and the sense of freedom is empowering, plus your balls will be enjoying plenty of action.

The Dating Game

Since I began my quest to enlighten and educate the bumbling fools that I see annoying the beautiful – and not so beautiful ladies of Ireland every weekend, I would like to think that I have passed on more than a few gems of wisdom. On deeper reflection, perhaps because of the skills set that I have developed over the years, maybe I've been expecting too much of the average man on the street, so I need to go back to basics and break down the crazy world of dating.

Here's a golden rule for dating – lads – ask birds out on dates. That might sound oversimplified, but generally the best ideas are the simplest ones. I love going on dates, if the bird is sound, chances are you're going to have a decent night, and more than likely get your hole, speaking from personal experience at least. We have all spent our formative years watching American TV shows and movies, watching the ups and down of the dating lives of Ross and Rachel, Buffy and Spike, Eric and Sookie, Blair and Chuck, JD and Elliot – not always the most conventional relationships but you get the idea. Despite so many aspects of

American culture permeating Irish society, dating has never truly caught on.

Once you embrace the fact that every date isn't going to turn into a relationship, you're ready to get dating. Instead of texting a bird saying "going out with the lads later, might see ye after the club" it's hardly going to require a change of knickers is it? If you ask her out on a date, those knickers will hopefully be on your bedroom floor the following morning. I honestly believe that anticipation is the greatest of all human emotions, therefore by giving her notice of your intention to take her out, you are not only making her feel special about herself, but makes your imminent hook up feel a lot more special than a drunken fumble in the smoking area of your favourite haunt.

Here are a few solid tips for first dates:

Don't set the bar too high; if you go all out on the first date and splash the cash she'll always be expecting the same – if not better. The pub for a drink is more than enough; restaurants can be daunting if you're a novice, best build up to it slowly.

Bowling

Bowling can actually be a fun date, you don't have to get too dressed up, so you see early on what she's like most of the time. With make-up and push-up bras, it's often impossible to accurately judge a woman until she rolls over the morning after.

Attend a Sporting Event

With the amount of jersey chasers on the go, this one is a winner. Obviously if you can get her All-Ireland final tickets when her county features – your lad will be like Kim Kardashian's latest Instagram, she'll be all over it.

Comedy Gig

I'm a massive fan of this one; a good gig puts both of you in good form and allows you to gauge her sense of humour. Believe it or not there are birds out there that don't appreciate the Player humour, obviously it's best to ditch these craic vacuums at the earliest opportunity.

Cinema

I know most people say this is a terrible idea, but it's fine, particularly if it's an online date, it cuts down on awkward conversation, if she turns out to be a swamp donkey at least you're in the dark and you get to see a movie and you can leg it straight away.

Dating is a bit of fun and a means to an end, for me this end is getting the ride, for most people it's a relationship. Going on a date, regardless of what you do: dinner; cinema; going for a quiet drink; going to the local strip club (oh yes I did), gives you an opportunity to get to know the other person much better than a drunken screaming match in a dingy nightclub. Not only do you learn about the person, the more dates you go on the better idea you have of what kind of partner you are actually looking for in the long run.

The only flaw in my plan is that Irish women sometimes are a disaster but that's another day's work.

The Sunday Game

S o the first date is over, now it's time to analyse events in the cold light of day. Away from the excitement of the occasion, the alcohol and the adrenalin have left the system; a clearer picture can now emerge. No harm in talking to a friend about it, sometimes within a few sentences your friend will be able to tell you what you were afraid to admit to yourself. You need to break the date down to get a true insight, discuss both side's tactics, style, any key turning points, was there any clear cut scoring opportunities? What you need is a Colm O'Rourke type friend here, sensible laid back and balanced, someone that's seen and done it all, there's no point in getting all excited by a Joe Brolly type, who'll have you getting down on one knee the next time you see her or telling you to ignore her so hard she'll begin to doubt her own existence.

What you need to look at areas like – was there genuine attraction? Women are wired differently to us blokes as we know, and it can take up to three dates for genuine attraction to build for the fairer sex and months to truly fall in love, with men we fall in lust pretty quickly, generally depending on what you're

44

wearing and bra size. If you don't want to kiss her within two hours in the romantic sense not the 'it's half two you'll do' kind of way, then forget about it. Attraction is like alcohol - like it or not - it's generally needed at some point to create the lubrication of the path to romantic endeavours.

As I always say they're all nice when they're new, what you find cute and endearing now could drive you crazy in a few months. Her 'funny' laugh could eventually sound like nails on a blackboard when the honeymoon period is a distant memory. We choose to ignore many faults in others, initially due to the excitement of a new romance, like buying shoes that are that bit tight but were on sale so you couldn't not get them. You love them at first but soon they cause nothing but pain and discomfort. I'm not saying you should dump a girl because she supports Liverpool (although I have) or because she ate the food on her plate in alphabetical order (happened to one of the lads) or because instead of laughing she just said "that's so funny" (me again). All I'm saying is be aware of her idiosyncrasies from the outset.

Shopping when you're hungry is a bad idea, as is dating when you're lonely; you'll end up regretting what you're stuck with. You need to be in a good place yourself, otherwise you won't attract the calibre of bird you deserve. I know lads that put more effort into picking their fantasy football teams than into relationships they are about to enter.

Communication is a massive part of being in a relationship, which essentially means having to listen to her. The only time I want to listen to a bird moan is when I'm giving her a good seeing too. I don't want to hear about what her friend said or who was wearing what the other night. I find it hard to believe that women actually think that guys listen to them for any other reason than to get into her knickers. As for the dramas over absolutely nothing, "I'm never taking to her again because she didn't answer my phone call. Blah blah blah"! Not forgetting the torture of heading out with her hot friends, the frustration of not being able to flirt with, or score them is too much for me. Girlfriends are such cock blocks.

I don't get why you'd go out if you have a bird. When I go out the possibilities are endless. Everyone is fair game, I'm like Real Madrid, I can have whoever I want whenever I want. The best part of being single is the thrill of the chase, why would you give that up? A different woman every night is the way to go. "Sex without love is an empty experience" they say but as empty experiences go it's a good one!

Top sportsmen often visualise the result they want from a particular shot to help them achieve success, have you done this? Generally, once a bird gets comfortable in the relationship you're in trouble. The pounds pile on, she stops shaving her legs, the sexy lingerie disappears to be replaced by Bridget Jones' type knickers. Your FHM collection will be replaced by *Cosmo*. You'll be hanging out with her sisters instead of the lads. The closest you'll get to a three-way is if you share the bed with her teddy bear. If you have taken all this on board and are happy to proceed then go for it.

From a practical point of view you need to have a relationship check list:

1. Does this lady possess the qualities that are important to you in a potential partner?

2. Have you considered the purpose of this relationship for both of you? Fun, marriage, company, other.

3. Are you physically and sexually attracted to this person?

4. Do you mind missing important matches going forward?

5. Does watching soaps and reality television appeal to you?

6. Are you ok with being unable to chat up attractive ladies on a night out?

7. Are you prepared to curtail farting in bed until you're very comfortable together?

8. Do you enjoy following somebody around a shop without being able to check out the talent working there?

9. Have all the lads met her and had a proper look through her Facebook pictures first?

10. Have you considered getting a puppy instead?

The puppy option is a pretty solid one. Unfortuately due to my hetic social schedule I'm far too busy to properly care for man's best friend, however if I did want to spend all my time with a demanding high maintenance whiner, I'd get a dog. Bring it for walks, buy it a few toys, feed it well and more often than not she's still wants more whereas your canine friend will be wagging its tail with joy.

Why You're Single

Honesty is a very important part of dating. Obviously I don't mean being honest with your date – that'll never get you anywhere, being true to yourself is key. It's all well and good deciding that you want to meet somebody, but first you need to ask yourself why you're single. This can be pretty tough for most of us, asking friends is generally as pointless as asking a girl if her friend is hot. Unsurprisingly, friends will sugar-coat your deficiencies enough to give you diabetes if you swallow their fairytales.

If you are told any of the following things this is what your friends are actually trying to tell you:

You're Too Good to Settle

Basically you're extremely fussy and have an outrageously high opinion of yourself. Looking in the mirror you see a Michelle Keegan lookalike, in reality you're more like Kevin Keegan. You believe you appear aloof and mysterious on a night out, but this actually comes across as bitchy or arrogant which means you get less attention than the Sudoku in the *Sun* newspaper. Bin the ridiculous checklist and stop closing yourself off to the good ones. Yes, potential partners are like buses, they won't stop unless there's some kind of sign telling them they should.

You're Really Quirky

When your friends tell you that you're different, and that you need to meet someone that gets you, it means that you're about as much fun as standing barefoot on a piece of lego. Your attempt to cover up poor social skills and any spark of interest in your life isn't working. Dressing like a colour blind, homeless person or an obsession with only eating food that begins with C might make you stand out, but chronic flatulence does that too. Trust me, the quirks that suitors find adorable at the start turn sour faster than listening to Christmas music in shops in November. I'm not saying that we should all be carbon copies but don't be the Jim Corr of your group.

There's Nobody Decent Left

In my experience there's a few reasons for thinking this, for one you could have a face that would drive rats out of a barn and a personality that'd make Obama think "No we can't". Another reason ladies, is that you've dismissed the advances of so many decent lads for being too nice, that there is now a suburb in your town call Friendzone. Strangely the number of couples that seem to meet when he accidentally stumbles into her living-room while she's in her flannel pj's at 8pm watching the soaps, remains relatively low. If you don't put yourself out there how the hell will you meet someone? Try online dating, blind dates, taking up a class, something that helps you extend your social circle.

Haven't Found Your Type Yet

At least nobody is questioning your commitment to the quest for happiness; unfortunately you're as hopeless at searching for talent as the judges on *The Voice*. While you are looking for Prince Charming, you are prepared to kiss a few frogs along the way. Sadly you seem to be working your way through a procession of wasters that even Jeremy Kyle wouldn't touch. You're the kind of person that needs a project and despite the advice of friends, you think you can fix this guy or girl. Enthusiasm and unwavering belief that the next one will be THE one, that'd put any Mayo GAA fan to shame, simply proves that you haven't learned from past mistakes and perhaps a spell on the sidelines may provide fresh perspective.

You're Too Nice

The word nice is no longer a compliment; the English language is dripping with adjectives that can accurately convey positivism. If a meal is 'nice' it wasn't terrible, that's how I see it. As I always say – nice guys finish themselves off! The thrill is in the chase and if you don't put up any kind of challenge then you remove the thrill. Sure we see so-called nice guys with girls all the time, but the technical term for this is settling. How many people out there would honestly rather have someone in their lives as friends instead of confessing their feelings and possibly making both of you much happier? It's easier said than done, but is there anything worst than unrequited feelings? Like your bank balance – it's better to know exactly what's available to you.

What I would suggest is doing your very own SWOT analysis. See my own one as an example. I find these particularly useful in a wide range of situations as long as you fill them in honestly, as

I have. Have a go at it, maybe you'll realise you're as boring as a Tuesday night in Athlone and that personal development is the first step you need to take. You can have the nicest pub in the world, but if the drink is warm or leaves a bitter taste, it won't attract the kind of discerning customers you want. A few new shirts could be worth missing a couple of unsuccessful nights out for, changing from Lynx Africa to an expensive aftershave may be a game changer too – who knows?

Galway Player SWOT Analysis

Internal	
Strengths	**Weaknesses**
Ridiculously good looking	As loyal as a premiership footballer
Charming	
Amazing in bed	Scored most of the best birds in Galway already
Confident	
Stylish	Small bit of a reputation
Physique sense of humour	
Conversation skills	Commitment issues (apparently)
Intelligence	
Social status	
Financial stability	
External	
Opportunities	**Threats**
Models/TV Presenters	~~Younger guys~~
Tourists	~~STI~~
Twitter followers	~~Disgruntled boyfriends~~
New birds turning 18 every day	~~Knocking a bird up~~
	~~Getting a girlfriend~~

Your SWOT Analysis

Internal	
Strengths	**Weaknesses**

External	
Opportunities	**Threats**

Friendzone

So where is the most depressing place in the world to live? No, not the Midlands – it's actually a place called the 'Friendzone'. It's a place occupied by nice guys or losers, or as I call them, saps. The Friendzone is similar to a complex sexual Bermuda triangle for many men. They do what they can to get close to a bird, think they're on the right track to bangtown, then all of a sudden she's telling you that you're like a brother to her and she's pouring her heart out to you about some total bastard that she's crazy about.

Once in the dreaded Friendzone, it can be very hard to get out, the best way to get out is – never to be in it in the first place! When you first meet a bird socially, make sure that she is fully aware of your intentions, be on the edge, show her your dangerous side. Always make cheeky flirty comments and touch her inappropriately, breaking down her defensive system. As I always say, it's a numbers game and some guys will see this as over the top. Sure I get blown off plenty, but I also get blown plenty.

We all know guys who are constantly in this state of sexual purgatory. But why do they always end up there? There are a few red flags that these guys should be aware of, such as The Dream Date, i.e. he's dreaming if he ever thinks he'll ever pull her. Some girls are just out of your league, deal with it. Like Liverpool fans thinking this will be their year, it's just not going to happen. There are girls that just aren't into you, just give up and move on. Another common mistake is being infatuated with one particular girl, there are thousands of hot girls in Galway (and plenty of mingers) so why get hung up on one? They put this girl on a pedestal and no girl can ever compete with his idealist and generally misguided ideas of this lady. This is one case where friends are very important, they need to help the poor unfortunate see the wood for the trees.

A fatal error and a key reason why these muppets never get the girl, is that they never make a move. The main reason for this is fear of rejection and the fear of ruining the friendship. Often fear of success is our biggest obstacle not a fear of failure. You have to put things into perspective here, getting your hole is more important than having female friends.

So if you are in the Friendzone how do you get out? Some guys think the Friendzone is a backdoor into a woman's affections. Stop dreaming, your life isn't a romcom. Once you're firmly residing in this land of the hapless, you have nothing to lose except her friendship, but what's the point in being friends with a girl that won't put out. It's like having a Ferrari in the driveway and not being able to drive.

A few things you can do to escape is to make her jealous, tell her in graphic detail about your conquests, real or imaginary. Give yourself the upper hand by rejecting her sexually; tell her that you just want to be friends, that she's not your type, reverse all the junk you've been told all your dating life. Don't be her lapdog; ignore her calls for a few days. If all that doesn't work, well she's just not that into you and you're a loser!

Don't get me wrong I have plenty of female friends, but most of these are smoking babes that I've nailed and we're mates now. It's important to have female allies, but at least in this instance we both know where we stand. If you think about it, these guys who claim to be happy just being friends with girls they secretly adore, are actually liars, at least I'm honest and open, when I meet a bird I tell her I want to bang her like a barn door in a hurricane and more often than not it makes everyone happy.

Nice guys are a lot like Trocaire boxes, you're happy to have it around, think about it every now and again and regret not giving it more attention once it's gone. Women love a bad boy because they think that they can change him and because of the basic human desire of always wanting what you can't have. Relationships with so called bad boys are generally one dimensional, leaving the need for real sharing, caring communication and emotional intimacy unfulfilled. This is where the saps come in, the dependable losers who reply to text messages immediately, that are thoughtful, caring and genuine and pick up the slack. By the way, bad boys aren't actually that bad they just couldn't care less about you, so their mysterious and moody behaviour is apathy, selfishness and avoidance tactics.

A friend of mine was recently told if he was a dickhead the girl he coveted would be far more inclined to engage in a relationship, but nothing would transpire because he was too nice. As ridiculous as this sounds, it's a common occurrence, nice guys are turning into women and giving women a dangerous ascension into the previous unchallenged male domain of hunter-gatherer. Dating is complicated enough without the tradition lines being blurred. Lads, look between your legs, that thing means you're the boss!

Guys, my advice is simple, grow a pair and face the fact that 'nice guys not only finish last, they finish themselves off'. Follow my example, take her down off that pedestal and be more like yours truly, see women for what they really are – something to be enjoyed and used – they are complicated and illogical, so until you find one that you can half put up with – enjoy playing the field.

Hilariously, the last time I discussed this topic I caused quite a stir, with every white knight and troll online highly offended by my blunt assertions. In the ensuing online, newspaper and radio debates, not one person was able to offer an argument other than the fact that I was a bastard, something I fully agree with. My life and everything that I have seen in dating with my own two eyes, in addition to the countless research I've read, continues to prove my point.

Torres Syndrome

Going through a prolonged dry spell can be a major worry. Your confidence deserts you faster than a record label drops the average *X Factor* winner and you start thinking that you'll never score again. We've all been there, I remember at one stage in 2011 when I went three weeks without any action, I still break out in cold sweats just thinking about it. The more you think about it and talk about it, the bigger the problem seems until you eventually become your own cock block.

Fear not, there is help out there. The boring experts will give you the same old tips, change your wardrobe, try new places to head out, sign up for online dating. These are all as obvious as the nose on Zlatan Ibrahimovic's face, what you need to do is think outside the box. The best advice I can offer is to bed an absolute hound. Lowering your standards until you regain your mojo will have the desired effect, particularly if you are discreet about your conquests. You don't want word spreading that your standards are slipping or you'll have all kind of mutts sniffing round you.

I'm talking about the kind of girl that the only time she sees a cock is when she's having her cereal in the morning. She gets less action these days than Bebo. Tell yourself that this is like a friendly in football – it's just preparation for more important games ahead. The reality is that girls that don't get that much action are better in bed, they try far harder. Older, uglier birds put in extra effort knowing that the next ride could be her last. This is the perfect time to experiment and add to your repertoire.

Heading out with someone on a hot streak is always advisable, watching his body language, listening to the conversations he starts, even the types of girls he goes for can be the boost you need to help you click back into winning ways.

Trying too hard is always a turn off too. The smell of want is never very attractive and can become a genuine stumbling point. Your first thought on a night out should be to go out and enjoy yourself with your mates and let the rest take care of itself, playful flirting during the night lays foundations, but having fun is the number one priority. In fact, sometimes it helps to tell yourself that you genuinely don't want to pull, that you're just out for the laugh. You often hear commentators saying the striker missed a glorious chance because he had too much time to think, when instincts take over – we can become less successful becaue we overthink an opportunity.

I remember reading somewhere that the best way to motivate yourself when you are struggling romantically is to watch Romcoms. Turn on *The Notebook, An Officer and a Gentleman* or *Love Actually* and this will sort you out. That's like recommending a diet of cake to help a fat person lose weight, absolute nonsense! Romcoms generally have the opposite effect - if you take them seriously you will spiral into a stupor of hopelessness and hang up your trusted lucky jocks.

The reality is that women go through the same experiences of unfulfillment, maybe we need to set up a group for people experiencing similar problems, who may or may not wish to help each other out. There's nothing to be ashamed of, if people were more open about their feelings, there would be a lot more sex in the world and a lot more people walking around with a smile more often.

Define Girlfriend

The start of a relationship is a fascinating time, with endless possibilities and questions, hopes and dreams. It's a wonderful time in anyone's life, I just worry that some people get distracted in the early days. It takes a good few dates to really get to know a bird, so I think it's always important to keep your options open. If you have a half-decent bird, you may as well keep her onside until you find someone better. As I always say "a bird in the bed is worth two in the club".

Some guys worry about cheating, or think it's wrong – nonsense, perfection is an endless aspiration, we all want the perfect woman, by two timing, we are simply using our valuable time more efficiently. Dating back to prehistoric times, the male species was given a genetic imperative to spread their seed among as many females as possible to ensure the survival of the human race. It's in our DNA.

A personal observation is – most cases of cheating could be prevented if ladies upped their own game, tone up, cut out the mood swings, push the envelope in the bedroom … it's just a thought.

Anyway guys, if your lady friend is going to last, you need to know that she can be moulded into your way of thinking from the outset. Hence extra curricular activities from the outset, can be a valuable tool in assessing your compatibility. Cheating or keeping your options open – as I like to call it, is like getting into a steaming hot bath – you don't dive right in or you'll get burned, ease yourself in gently and deliberately take extra care around the genital area.

Because putting a label on your relationship status is such a big deal for birds, it gives you ample opportunity to play the field until after you are actually titled boyfriend (and afterwards too if you want). Here are a few tips that I've learned throughout my career that will ensure that you keep out of trouble:

Don't let her get into a habit of texting you 24/7, convince her that you're not much of a texter and that this kills the spark in any relationship. Make her think that if you're not in constant contact you'll have much more to talk about when you meet up, and that couples who are updating each other are losers who won't last. Try to minimise communication to texts, text message is much easier to conceal than a phone call if you're on another date. You can hide the content of a message on any decent phone. I always save birds that I am seeing by their initials and have a male name to substitute 'So when AK texts it's Alan Keane texting you not Áine King'. Always delete your messages too, most people lock their phones but women are sneaky and I've caught more than one chick looking through my outbox.

You have to be savvy on your laptop too, anything pertaining to your philandering should be stored in a folder called Fantasy Football. This includes hiding your private internet browser for your POF account, etc.

Avoid photos and facebook check-ins like the plague; it's currently the biggest barrier to effective monogamy circumvention.

It's so true to say, we are the generation where deleting history is more important than making it.

Socialising is obviously a key element to any relationship, keeping you dating venues parallel, never ever mix and match, because some jealous barman or cock blocking bitch could ruin one or all of your relationships. On nights out, don't try too hard to impress her mates, be like Glen Whelan or Keith Andrews in the Irish midfield – you know they're out there giving it socks for ninety minutes, but nobody really takes any heed of them unless they score or get a card. If a bird brings you out to meet her friends you're in, so relax focus on her, in an ever shrinking world it's best to keep your head down, blend in, and you're much less likely to get caught while your doing your research.

A friend in need is a must, it has to be someone she has met and you use this person as your get out clause when you're meeting your other bit of fluff. It's an airtight alibi once he's fully briefed on proceedings, it's particularly ingenious because you only stand her up to be a good friend and soon any failing of yours can be vented vicariously through your loser mate who is going to be the subject of all of her fire most of which should be directed at you.

I'm not advocating relationship spuriousness merely for the sake of it, I guess I'm a romantic at heart and I think the search for true love should never stop because of silly little issues, like girlfriends or monogamy.

Interesting Interests

Let's be honest, roaring and shouting at someone, fuelled by the pubs break-even point in alcohol sales, isn't necessarily the perfect way to meet someone. As a dating guru, I'm always being asked what's the best way to meet someone. You need to put yourself out there, sitting in watching *Match of the Day* every Saturday night or having a wine night with the girls may be fun, but unless the pizza boy/girl is a beaut, and your life is like the script of a badly written porno, it's not going to help you meet someone.

You need to think outside the box to get into one, if you catch my drift. I have found social media has greatly increased my social circle. I attend numerous Networking Events for like-minded individuals. One of the most enjoyable is the 'Into the West Bloggers Network', basically I saw this event on twitter, rocked into the G Hotel in Galway one Saturday afternoon, I was the only guy amongst twenty three lovely ladies, you don't need to be blessed with my skills to flourish in this environment.

I've always maintained that you can tell a lot about a man by the hobbies and interests he has, if you've ever played a team sport, it gives you a great grounding in life. Hobbies are a wonderful way to meet like-minded people and a way to express your creative side. A shared passion can bring people together, sport for example is almost unparalleled in this area, look at the Irish team under Jack Charlton – our qualifications for Euro 88 and Italia 90 are cited as some of the main catalysts for the Celtic Tiger Economy such was their effect on the population.

Men for the most part, have plenty of hobbies, which is one of the main reasons that we are the more level-headed sex. Being able to deal with the rollercoaster of emotions that your favourite team puts you through every Saturday afternoon helps to put the ups and downs of life into perspective. Essentially, if women had more interests and hobbies outside gossiping and complaining, the world would be a much better place. Any woman, for example, that follows the Premier League or the Six Nations wouldn't be getting so excited over her man leaving the toilet seat up.

While doing my research for this article, I asked a number of ladies to list their hobbies and girls I've got news for you – walking, watching soaps, shopping, going out and going to the cinema are not hobbies, they are things you do, none of which are particularly interesting – especially the soaps one, think about it, you're not going to read a report on last night's episode of *Fair City* on the back page of any newspaper tomorrow are you?

I also encountered a cohort of ladies who claimed to have certain interests which were merely poor attempts to impress me. Birds who claim to like video games, cars or any sport, to share her guy's interests – the sentiment is nice but misguided. Jane Austen in *Pride and Prejudice* could very well have been referring to women's knowledge of sport when she wrote, "Mary wished to say something very sensible, but knew not how." This lack of know-how leads to arguments – another weakness of the fairer sex (dealing with fights). Fear not folks, as ever I am here with a sensible resolution which will be agreeable to all parties, I believe.

I have devised a number of hobbies which ladies can enjoy but which will also make them a more attractive prospect to men.

Pole Dancing

Great for fitness and a terrific conversation piece on a date, trust me.

Hot Yoga

Improves flexibility and gets guy's minds racing, fit women in skimpy outfits dripping with sweat.

Cooking

We all know the way to a man's heart is through his stomach, it doesn't have to be too fancy, but a willingness to experiment will bring it's own rewards.

Lap Dancing

Okay, most types of dancing, but this in particular as dancing is a vertical expression of a horizontal desire, plus it can be a great way of earning good money if you fall on tough times.

Knitting/Sewing

Not the sexiest hobby on the list, but someone has to do it and it's not going to be me.

Massages

Nothing better than a good rubdown after a tough day by hands that know what they're doing, nobody want a massage that make them feel like they've just gone 12 rounds with Muhammad Ali.

Modelling

Trust me if you drop this into the conversation, no lad will complain and it looks like great fun.

It's not rocket science, an interesting hobby will make you stand out from the crowd and give you a better chance of him actually calling you, especially if this hobby improves your nocturnal abilities.

One very social sport which has exploded in popularity over the recent years, is Tag Rugby. As a sport I'm indifferent as a concept, yet it has to be one of the most important innovations in the singles scene since the invention of lying. A mixed sport, which awards three points for a female try – as opposed to one for the more common male score, thereby artificially inflating the importance of women and thus sustaining their interest throughout the season. Any normal man will have grown up playing sport and will have shared some of the greatest moments of his youth on the local playing fields, with male comrades. Remember any big win and the celebrations you've enjoyed afterwards – now substitute Niall the flatulent cornerback, for Nicola the hot winger, and those nights out and celebrations suddenly become much more interesting and enjoyable.

My favourite feature of the season is seeing what sexbomb I'll be tackling from week to week. The phenomenal standard at the

Galway venue ensures that every team has at least one babe, with more on the better selected teams. This is a solid fact, a few of the lads and I have assessed every team in the league.

These type of women are fascinating also, ranging from:

The Princess

Who is there to be seen, with perfectly applied make-up and spend less time on the field than your average TD spends in the Dáil.

Mucksavages

Who relish the chance to get stuck into tackles and are as happy to go through you as around you. Probably plays GAA herself and always wanted to get to take on the lads.

The Meerkat

Always looking around checking out who's about, the type of girl that is on Plenty of Fish, she's not desperate, but willing to go out of her comfort zone to meet a guy, even if it means getting steamrolled by an over zealous overweight opponent.

Dummies

They already have boyfriends, I don't really understand why they play, taking up valuable space on the field. I've actually approached the organisers about getting them to ask women to wear different colour tags depending on their relationship status, I haven't got a reply yet, but hopefully it's something they'll take on board for next season.

As I say it's the ideal place to meet someone, if you fancy a bird when she's wet, dirty and sweaty … well you know where I'm going with that. The nights out after games are brilliant, a few cheeky comments during a game are the key to a successful night out, with discussions of ball handling, stamina, scoring ability and big tackles, always enjoyable. I actually asked a smoking hot babe out during a game once; despite her terrible footwear, her attempts to resist my charms off the pitch were as futile as her attempts to prevent me scoring on it.

Guys can substitute the normally genius chat-up line "So where are ye from?" Instead they can ask "How did ye do?" Maybe it's not too late to retire those check shirts and try on some velcro shorts and give everyone a break from the tired mating rituals we witness every weekend in our pubs and clubs.

Dancing King

ew people realise that when George Bernard Shaw uttered the immortal phrase, "Dancing is a vertical expression of a horizontal desire", he was actually bemoaning his experience with a multi-Feis winning, Irish dancer. Most people upon hearing the phrase, immediately think of the most sensual dances: the Tango, Flamenco, Waltz or Twerking. However, as skilful as Irish dancing is, and despite the best efforts of Michael Flatley & Co, if all those dances were a group of girls you'd describe Irish dancing as the one with a 'great personality'.

People don't realise the deep psychological trauma suffered by Ireland's female population due to the Irish dancing lessons of their youth. A fear of intimacy, an addiction to fake tan, an over dependency on hair extensions ... these are just some of the side effects suffered by Mná na hÉireann. In fact, the persistent drone of 'One-two-three' bellowed out by angry middle-aged women, seems to be a subliminal binary type code which has programmed generations of Irish women. My research shows the asexual moves required for the performances, has indeed in far too many cases, sadly, stayed with the pupils. The rigid upper body, hands stuck to the sides and a face on her like an Irish

Rugby fan at the final whistle of the Ireland New Zealand game, tragically aren't left behind when they hang up their pomps.

Undoubtedly, the average Irish man also has his issues when it comes to tripping the light fantastic. 'Nobody puts Baby in the corner' or a sober Irish man on the dancefloor. Despite knowing that there are few better ways to impress the fairer sex, Irish men still face a fear of taking to the dance floor on a par with Joey Essex's fear of reading educational material. Unlike refining your performance for the no pants dance which is both fun and beneficial, wayward attempts to dance can be crushing for Irish men. Most expeditions to the dance floor are alcohol fuelled, with the resulting flashbacks leaving mental scars that'll cause cold sweats if they even accidentally land on *Strictly*.

Some to their eternal credit, believe they are John Travolta in *Saturday Night Fever,* but to an outsider, their efforts resemble a demented Davy Fitz on the sidelines squealing for a free. In defence of my brethren, while the girls were sent off to Irish dancing classes, we were sent to the local sports grounds. Sadly the range of movement required to achieve success on the local GAA pitch is not especially transferable to the dance floor. Having said that, we all know those who earnestly endeavour to replicate some of their trademark moves, particularly the shoulder charge and in some cases, depending on whether he has the good jeans on or not, sliding tackles.

So here goes girls – try to loosen up – both vertical and horizontal dancing should be a full body experience. Lads, instead of grinding up against her like a fleabitten tomcat rubbing up against a pebbledashed wall, practice a few simple moves and dance like nobody is watching. After all, a dance before going out to score seems to be working out pretty well for the All Blacks.

Lie to me...

I get asked on a regular basis by guys if it's okay to trick girls into liking you. It's hard to believe that this would ever even enter someone's mind. Questioning whether using deception and prepared routines to alter a person's perception and ultimately win their affection, seems bizarre to me. How are we ever going to get what we desire unless we massage the truth and tell people what they want to hear? We do this successfully in every walk of life, so why not in the dating world? White lies are just as much a part of every day conversation as body language and tone.

A date is a lot like a job interview, without the sex at the end – well depending what the interview was for. Basically, you need to present your best side, tell them what they want to hear and create a connection. Without going to this effort you're about as appealing as an away trip to Germany for a Spanish side. Unlike perspective employers, women are generally much less intimidating and much easier to mislead, thereby speeding up the natural order of modern dating, Lie, Lie & Bye (Lie to, Lie with and Say Bye).

According to my own very scientific research, the average person has seven relationships during their life. Since you can only actually have one successful relationship, why not engage in a few practice ones? I'm not saying to enter a relationship to deliberately hurt someone, just don't be expecting every girl you date to be the one. In this spirit we are akin to politicians, realistically they are good people, we all hear the tripe about broken promises, but in reality their hands are tied whilst in administration, despite their best efforts, it can be difficult to deliver the promises they made on the door step, unfortunately if they came to you and said, "I'm going to do my best, but in all honesty I may not be very effective," you are simply not going to vote for them. Transfer this to dating and be very honest on your first date, let's see how far that gets you!

I once dated a dog lover, I had to borrow a friend's white Maltese puppy every time she was calling over, because to woo her I had claimed to own the mutt. While the girl was pretty entertaining for a while, my canine wingman's capacity to urinate more than your average racehorse was a deal breaker, my apartment was starting to smell like I shared it was a homeless person (wino). The point is, I used a prop to meet someone, ultimately it went nowhere, but there was no harm done, except to my Kodari rug which I had to throw out.

The worst thing about dating is having to pretend that you like to do other things besides sex, drinking and watching sport, telling a date the truth will ensure you have plenty of time for the latter of that trio but get none of the first.

Telling people what they want to hear is a skill, some guys excel at it, but believe me it's not just guys that like to bend the truth. Here are some of the biggest lies that girls tell guys.

I'm Not Ready for a Relationship

She's not ready for a relationship with you, to be precise. Some guys are like a McDonald's meal, you think it's exactly what you want but you shortly after having it you still feel unsatisfied. The trick to winning her affections, is to tell her that you don't want a relationship, particularly not with her. Ignoring her for extended periods also works a treat.

I Don't Care How Much You Earn

What she really means here is how the hell you are going to support your children and her shoe addiction on the minimum wage? Women are forward thinkers, men use the Premiership fixtures to track time, women use their biological clocks. Being a woman is a competitive business, so when she's describing you to the girls, she needs to be able to sell you. Male friends just look at a girl's Facebook profile picture before offering approval, her girls may stop short of Garda vetting.

I Never Normally Do This

She just doesn't want you to think she's easy, which she obviously is. Just reassure her that you don't either but it's different with her, you feel a real connection or some other nonsense. Recent surveys show that two thirds of Irish women have had one night stands, with a fifth of women sleeping with someone whose name they didn't even know. Thankfully attitudes towards sex have changed in Ireland. Sexual compatibility is critical to a happy relationship, therefore it makes sense to establish whether you have a connection right from the start.

I Dress for Myself - Not to Impress a Man

This is only half a lie, women spend more time worrying about what other girls think of their outfit rather than what a guy will think of it. If you're showing plenty of leg, cleavage or both, guys will like your outfit, end of. Women on the other hand, have an internal hard drive which stores information like how often she wore that outfit before, how much it cost, where she got it. The only answer this incredible fashion catalogue can't provide is 'Who does she think she is?'

I Don't Want a Bastard - I Want a Nice Guy

Still the ultimate lie that women tell us and themselves. Speaking from first hand experience, I can solemnly tell you this is nonsense. Women love the challenge of a bad boy and the emotional rollercoaster it guarantees. Being unpredictable and playing by your own rules is the ultimate aphrodisiac. I've said it before and I'll say it again, "Treat them mean keep them keen".

He Text Me

Lads that little thing in your trousers, or in my case extremely large thing, can be the most important factor in determining your success with a new girl. Mobile phones and all they allow us to do have never been as integral in the dating game. A polished phone game is now as important as style, looks, charm and a good sense of humour. With a whole host of ways to communicate, it's never been easier to stay in contact and perhaps destroy a relationship between meetings.

I'm too young to remember the dark old days Before Mobiles (BM) but there has been a seismic change on the dating landscape. Imagine ringing her home landline at 3am as drunk as a junior footballer the night before a game, looking for a booty call. Generations of young men sheepishly fingered the rotary dial on the old school phones praying herself answered, not the Irish Mammy with more awkward questions than the Leaving Cert Irish Orals, or worse still the auld lad whose little princess you were hoping to seduce.

It was a simpler time BM, communication was minimal, you lived your own life and had actual news when you got to converse as opposed to now:

As a rather reserved nation, dirty talk was never going to be our forté, which isn't really a surprise. A strict Catholic upbringing and being in a phone box at the end of your street with the nasally violating stench of last night's Guinness flavoured piss aren't exactly a renowned aphrodisiac. Beating 20p into the slot and speaking into a petrie bowl of every germ known to Science, and a few undiscovered ones, used to be the only contact between meetings. The big question is, was this better than the constant contact we enjoy/endure today?

Over analysis of guy's texts has now become one of the most popular pastimes amongst women, it's up there with changing their Facebook profile pictures and talking about going on diets.

"What do you think he means by this?" is the normal question I get, it's frequently exactly what he means. Most of the girls I know would put regarded scholars to shame, with an astonishing ability to interpret a text. An apparently innocent message can be a cry for help, a sign of a pending existential crisis which only you can save him from. It could always be the fact that he is actually busy or unhappy for completely independent reasons, like a soul crushing defeat at FIFA, you know – important stuff.

Texting is a crucial weapon in your dating arsenal. In a recent survey 78% of women admitted they preferred to be asked out by text. I recalled one Sunday night at home when my phone was bouncing around the table like an epileptic seal at a rave. Five different birds; past, present and future conquests were texting me. Like everything else regarding dating, I used my tried and tested techniques to keep everybody (mainly me) happy and here's how it's done:

When you are going to send a text wait about 10 minutes before you send it. It can be very difficult, to recover from a poorly constructed, impulsive message. Once you send a text, forget about it and don't hang around for the response, you're a busy man with plenty of options. Keep your texts brief, not as short as an ex of mine who was clearly on a plan – per word – not per text. Make your texts interesting and finish with a question. Don't always finish with a question though, simply answering her question can be a great test. If she replies with another line of conversation, you can be pretty sure that she's keen. Build up to asking her out, never do it in the first text, you'll come across as cocky and she'll feel devalued. Humour can be difficult to get right in early messaging unless you're a skilled scribe like me.

Women have an innate understanding of all this, like cooking, knitting and giving birth they just know how to do it, so you need to be savvy when replying to messages. She is generally sitting around in her pyjamas with a clan of diabolical evil text geniuses helping her, studying every last word, analysing the tone and reading between the lines, whereas most guys are half-watching a match and sending a half-arsed reply. As I've already said, don't reply immediately, but don't be predictable, vary the duration of your replies. Don't answer boring questions, make her work for your attention. It helps to create a yes ladder, it works for those annoying cold callers, so make it work for you.

Emojis yes or no? It's a serious debate that I'm not sure has ever been properly addressed heretofore. A picture paints a thousand words, so what does the little yellow face say about you: fun loving; cool; trendy or tragic; creepy and strange. ☺ ☺

My gut feeling is that they are like the fat friend; they shouldn't be your go to move, but if nobody else is looking and it helps you get out of a dry spell, go for it. If she is flat out sending smiles and winks then it's perfectly acceptable. Always aim to reply with as many or less than her. If you finish every text with a winky face, you might as well just download the chloroform and cloth icon.

I recall one young toned, tanned, feisty, beauty … sorry I got lost in a daydream there, good times! Anyway, one girl really got me thinking, not just about how amazing I am with women, but about how technology has become the third wheel in all of our romantic experiences. The night began like any other, I identified the lucky lady who would be the recipient of my affections for the night, I engaged her with my usual charm offensive and within minutes she was almost ready to hand me her French knickers and say "here you go, I won't be needing these tonight."

Oddly as the night wore on, I sensed that I would not be getting the opportunity to study this particular lady's bedroom ceiling that night. Undeterred, I stayed with her like a Galway GAA defender, not overly close, gently brushing up against her on occasion, but ultimately giving her plenty of room to express herself. She was obviously enjoying my company, hence one can only assume that she hadn't shaved her legs or there was a technical issue preventing my usual nocturnal formalities. Like a sunny day in Galway, some things are worth waiting for, this girl fell into that category.

The intriguing thing about this blonde bombshell, who had obviously had met plenty of players in the past, just none of my calibre, was her communication strategy. She insisted on not sharing full names or any form of social media contacts. In fact, my new friend went so far as to give me her landline number instead of mobile digits.

The following day I couldn't stop thinking about her. It was just that ass that you'd love to bounce a two euro coin off or her tempting cleavage, which I swear smiled back at me. I was thinking about all the nonsense that her approach eliminated.

Fed up playing games, second guessing Facebook check ins, tardy replies to Whats App messages, inane text tennis conversations, this girl was going old school. I have to admit that I too found it refreshing, actually hearing her voice and judging her mood and interest on the tone of her voice, not by the number of smilies in her texts. I could honestly see this genuinely working as a way to being in a relationship.

Obviously it didn't work for us, because I did find her on her Facebook and ended up doing one of her hotter friends I matched with earlier that night on Tinder, still it was worth a try …

Love Me Tinder

Online dating has evolved into an integral part of the dating landscape, like heavily padded bras, it's something we just have to make the most of and move on, there's no denying it provides a genuine alternative to the existing options. Now, thanks to the wonders of modern technology, you can get rejected from the comfort of your own living-room or meet the girl of your dreams whilst sitting on the jacks.

Ireland is a very small place with two degrees of separation, people are very conscious about being seen on a dating site. Heaven forbid people would find out that you're being proactive about meeting someone. Most proper Irish neighbours know what you had for breakfast anyway, so who cares what they think? We're not the fastest at accepting change in this part of the world, most new trends begin in America, come across the Atlantic, but a quick look at the Irish coast and they head straight for the continent or London.

The first stumbling block for most people is having to fill out their profiles. It's basically a quiz about yourself, yet astonishingly most people fail spectacularly. I guess the main question you have to ask yourself is "To Lie or Not to Lie?" Trust me you always lie, or as I like to think of it as, portraying yourself in the best possible light. Adding a couple of inches is always advisable (to your height that is), age is another one that you can play around with, it's only a number after all.

I have three different Plenty of Fish accounts, it's fascinating to see the different responses I get to the same questions from different accounts, often people just tell you what you want to hear. Some people are so dishonest ...

Let's be realistic here, when it comes to dating, looks are the deal breaker. The recent surge in population of dating app Tinder, apart from my endorsement, is due to the fact that it cuts straight to the chase. A strong selection of photographs is key, stay away from drunken group photos, or photos of you with a better looking friend or a hot girl. Personality is massively overrated, for most Irish relationships, you spend the initial periods together in a drunken-hangover haze or playing text tennis, sending each other the kind of rubbish that could ruin a man's reputation if they ever fell into the wrong hands. Physical attraction is the key to build a solid foundation in a relationship, in my experience.

One of the best compliments you can pay any successful new innovation is "Why didn't I think of that?" The beauty of Tinder is it's simplicity. Log on via Facebook, receive assurance that this will never appear on Facebook and away you go. Tinder can be considered a pain free version of what really happens on a night out. We mentally swipe everyone we see anyway, so why not give the option of turning this into an opportunity to engage in meaningless casual sex?

The straight version of Grindr, this Sexual Sat Nav is basically Facebook without all the stupid updates and annoying game invitations. I predominantly use Facebook to amuse my friends and to check out women. It's main use is essentially to see what mutual friends we have and if she's single or not. Tinder takes out all the hard work for you, if she's on here she's up for a bit of fun.

The advantage that it has over conventional dating sites, is that the only people who can contact you are those that you approve, if only we could have such a luxury on a night out.

A few tips to be successful on Tinder are:
- ✓ Always wait a few hours before messaging a match, you don't want to come across too keen.

- ✓ Don't be too persistent. If they don't reply to two messages in a row move on.

- ✓ Select attractive pictures of yourself, above all else this is how you are judged.

- ✓ If you're ugly have a good-looking friend in all your pictures to confuse possible suitors into thinking you're decent looking.

- ✓ Don't have a picture of yourself in a large group, with a member of the opposite sex, or a car as your profile or expect to get the flick.

- ✓ Only swipe on people you like, getting likes for the sake of it is as pointless as *X Factor*, it's completely contrived and leaves you feeling a little dead inside afterwards.

I have had hours of fun flicking through profiles with the lads, we even have developed a drinking game whereby you have to like everyone on it and you down a shot for every match, and a beer if she messages you first, and both if an ex messages you.

Dating sites have many benefits, most people online are open minded and looking to meet someone, so immediately you have common ground. A well-written profile means no shortage of conversation, yet some women I've come across still make the conversation more awkward than an interview with Brendan O'Connor. Some of the recent conversations I've had make me pity the future partner of these craic vacuums. Claiming that you want a guy with a good sense of humour, yet not appreciating my side splitting one liners – it's no wonder you're single ladies.

I'm considering opening a gym, from a quick glance on Plenty of Fish, it appears that roughly 98% of Irish women list going to the gym amongst their hobbies. I'm not sure what they do in these gyms as the vast majority aren't exactly a great advert for the place. No more than politicians' election posters, most of the birds online look like the before photos for a plastic surgery website.

On the subject of online dating, I've been thinking of creating a website to help all the lonely hearts out there. There's a lot of mutton dressed as lamb online, not to mention people whose profile bears less resemblance to reality than a playschool child's efforts. What I am proposing is www.RateMyDate.ie a site that allows you to rate your exes, divided into two sections.

First of all for the guys, birds can rate them out of ten on a number of categories:

- ✓ Neediness
- ✓ Sexual prowess
- ✓ Thoughtfulness
- ✓ Style
- ✓ Stamina
- ✓ Parenting potential

When it comes to rating ladies, the essential information lads need to know:

- ✓ Does she do one night stands?
- ✓ Appearance in the morning
- ✓ Open mindedness
- ✓ Flexibility
- ✓ Cooking skills
- ✓ Is she a moaner?

Imagine the amount of disastrous relationships that could be avoided with this site. I'll probably get a Nobel Prize for this and as the creator I will be exempt from mentions. It's the perfect site realistically.

When Sir Tim Berners-Lee invented the Internet 25 years ago, I doubt he could have dreamt that he'd enabled so many socially inept keyboard warriors to meet like-minded losers. Dating is a numbers game, so man up, cast out that rod and hopefully you get a nibble.

When Sally
Unfollowed Harry

"It was the best of times, it was the worst of times, it was the age of wisdom, it was the age of foolishness". I often wonder if Dickens was looking back to the French Revolution, or if indeed he was making a bold prediction about dating in the 21st century. We are blessed with incredible technology in every walk of life, all designed to making our lives easier and better, yet when it comes to dating, these advances have simultaneously made dating easier and trickier. Breaking up is never a pleasant experience and now thanks to social media, it's become even more testing and harder to move on.

Once burning a few photos and cinema ticket stubs was enough to cleanse the soul and start to mend a broken heart. Now you need a degree in software engineering and the stealth of the Russian Army to subtly conceal your dirty digital laundry. Changing your relationship status on Facebook is now one of people's biggest concerns when they curl up and sheepishly gawk at their future … alone. Imagine the great love stories if they had access to social media, If Noah's letters were anything to go by in *The Notebook*, can you imagine the nonsense he'd have been posting on his wall. Or when *Sally warned Harry* to: "try and find a way of not expressing every feeling you have, every moment that you have them" imagine if he was on Twitter, the film would be renamed: *When Sally Unfollowed Harry*.

Because our brains are wired from the beginning for bonding, breakups batter us biologically. "Initially," says Rutgers University anthropologist Helen Fisher, "everyone reacts to rejection like a drug user going through withdrawal." Given that there's a touch of a stalker in all of us, social media feeds this addiction. Scanning his pictures to see who he's chatting to, or where he's been photographed, checking her timeline to see how she's coping, it's simply too easy and not good for you. You can't move on if you don't let go, does that mean you shun all modern technology? Absolutely not, but tread carefully.

On reflection social media is a lot like alcohol. Treated with respect it can bring tremendous enjoyment and fun, but abused it can leave you in the horrors. When dealing with a break up, try to have perspective, don't bottle up your feelings, talk about it … to a real person not your computer.

Know the tweet that's one too many and please enjoy Facebook sensibly.

Text Mess

L ike sitting through a full episode of *Fair City*, no matter
how many times you have to draw the inevitable curtain
on a failed liaison, it doesn't get any easier. Relationships are
difficult enough at the best of times, so it only makes sense that
exiting is as painful as enduring them in the first place. As the
fat lady clears her throat, the only issue is how to bundle the
relationship into a canvas bag, add a few stones and throw it into
the nearest lake.

You rehearse your speech, drafting and redrafting, carefully
wording your thoughts, so as to cause minimum pain, yet clearly
get the message across, the other person always manages to make
things as awkward as seeing a woman driving with a man in the
passenger seat. Women are particularly adept at unsettling your
flow. They produce an assault on your efforts to separate, in a
fashion similar to the blanket defence used by GAA teams in
the North. They smother your natural game and force you into
ambitious and risky efforts. The inevitable waterworks will make
you end up losing your train of thought and ultimately saying
things that *can* and *will* be used against you in the future.

Having been through this on many occasions and having to listen to friends moan on about break-ups, I now genuinely believe that people need to accept that the best way to initiate a break up is via the planet's current most popular method of communication … text messaging. The amount of texts sent daily actually surpasses the number of personal interactions we have. The beauty of texting is that you don't have to witness the heartbreak you are causing first hand, the awkward silences, the overdramatic hyperventilation. Well-worded texts and limited replies will do the trick. It's not as if you want to stay friends with them after the break-up, so there's no onus on you to be nice to them here. In fact, it's giving them a clean break like pulling off a plaster and it helping them with the healing process by making them move on immediately.

People need to move with the times, texting and other forms of modern communications have being embraced when it comes to dating, but just because the break-up isn't as cool as the first kiss or the first date, shouldn't mean that we can't use the popular messaging service of the day to express the negative as well as the positive. In the past, people used *Dear John* letters and that was perfectly acceptable, so why do we get so much grief when it's a L8R John ☹ message?

The purpose of a break-up is to deliver a message. Texting is the most popular way of doing this right now. People will call this cruel but which is worse – that, or being confronted by a quivering mess and backtracking, or trying to soften the blow with some rhetoric which will give your former flame some fleeting hope when none exists? People please do the humane thing and press *send* to *end*.

The biggest question most people have when they're dumped is "Why?" So I've drawn up an exit survey if you will, for the dumper to fill out and help begin the healing process.

Break Up Survey

1	Was it me or you?	Me __	You __
2	Is there someone else?	Yes __	No __
3	Is this because _____ (insert own niggling doubt) _____?		

Please answer the following questions on a scale of 1-10:

1 being Very Dissatisfactory **10** being Extremely Satisfactory

Please rate your overall satisfaction with our relationship.	
How likely are you to recommend me to a friend seeking a relationship?	
How likely are you to return for a stay in the future?	
Compared to previous relationships how would you rate this one?	
Thinking about your overall experience, considering the emotional investment, do you feel this relationship was value for money?	

Overall Impression

We endeavour to offer the best possible experience to partners to help with future relationships, please rate based on the following criteria:

Overall service received	
Overall physical condition	
Exterior appearance	
Responsiveness to your needs	

The Ex Factor

S ome people just never learn!

I remember one particular Sunday session with the lads, swapping war stories about the night before, who got the most action and basically how lucky we are to be so good looking and so accomplished at being single – standard Sunday conversation to be honest.

The conversation somehow drifted into relationships and getting back with former lovers, one of the lads quite sheepishly defended the madness, it became quite apparent that he had got back with his ex. Schoolboy error. I know breaking up with someone is difficult. We've all been there, gutted, hoping the next text is from them, checking Facebook, Twitter, Foursquare, Bebo to see what's new with them. My advice in this sensitive time is build a bridge, get over it and blow the bridge up!

A break up can be tough to deal with, if you Google "how to get over a break up" there are over 3.19 million results. A lot of it is from so called relationship experts, some of them clearly know as little about break ups as Louis Walsh does about good music. My mother, a wise woman, has always told me that the best way to get over one woman is to get under another. That's easy for someone like me – but for the rest of you, here's a couple of things that may help you deal with your move to Loserville. Apparently listening to music can have a therapeutic effect on you, blasting out classics like *I will Survive* and *I Useta Lover* will definitely sort you out and ensure you stay single indefinitely. Often a chat with the lads after a break up will reveal their true feelings toward your ex, in a relationship it's difficult to be objective, so the lads are the best judge of her performance and can help ensure you don't repeat your mistakes.

Another tip that will keep popping up is that after you go through a break up you need to love yourself, now there are endless suggestions as to how you can do this, my suggestion is to do it literally, watch lots of porn to keep your mind off her and once you see all these hot birds on the internet, she'll pale in comparison.

People will argue that getting back with an ex can work and will scrape for examples to prove the point, but they are always the exception to the rule. You have to realise that people don't change, of course you can both make all kinds of promises, but it won't last, basically if you didn't get head the first time round she won't be going down now.

Women are like elephants they never forget, so if you did something wrong way back in the relationship, it will always be held against you.

One of the main reasons people consider getting back with an old flame is simply – loneliness, struggling to score on a night out, or a Saturday night in with nothing on TV except some soppy movie where a handsome multimillionaire ends up jetting into the sunset with a beautiful leading lady after a series of hilarious mishaps.

To ensure that you never make the ultimate mistake, I have a few suggestions such as drawing up a list of things you hate about her and accidentally e-mailing it to her, telling her that you have an STI, you could make a drunken pass at her mother, or my favourite would be to sleep with her best friend or her sister.

Sour Milk

The problem is that the single life is being undersold by the popular media. The agenda is being set by women, without a shadow of a doubt. You'd swear it was a disease! Most single people feel like they are on a waiting list, much like a transplant patient waiting for a new kidney. The constant cajoling to settle down and have that fairytale wedding isn't standard conversation for us men folk. The fact of the matter is, women peak before men, both in terms of maturity and looks wise, research suggests that ladies look their best in their 29th year, hence the rush to get hitched. On her special day every girl wants to look her best, and have less lines on her forehead than the first reading contains.

Given the likelihood of a relationship ending, particularly with an emotionally crushing and soul-destroying pain, I can't really see why it remains so popular. I'm told it's better to have loved and lost than never to have loved at all. I tell these people that they haven't had half enough one-night stands.

The problem is that most people are watching too many romantic comedies and listening to too much crap pop music. They are thinking with their heart not their head when it comes to relationships. Getting into a relationship is like taking a penalty, you need to have a cool head, decide on where you're going to stick it before you make your approach, aim low, but be prepared for shame and disappointment.

I can't help laughing when people tell me they've met *the one*. There was a time when FIFA 94 was the ultimate in soccer video gaming. I can still remember the awkward, blocky, difficult to control, girl that I used to go out with when I was a teen, what was I thinking? Remember you're first mobile phone, would you go back to that now? Not a chance, needs change, expectations change and most importantly people change.

What if your so-called soul mate, that one specific person out of the billions that have graced the planet, that one and only one person perfectly suited to you, turns out to be a thundering bitch? Imagine finding the one and she looks like a reject from the Irish *Take Me Out*. Or after years of searching you see him, and you just know, but he turns out to be a bigger prick than the spire. Of course this is okay for girls, as women for most of their single lives are subliminally attracted to bastards anyway.

It's vital that lads relax and savour they joys of single life. Given that men age like wine and women age like milk, I don't see any reason for a lad to get married under 30 years old at least. Older single men become like English soccer players; their value becomes massively inflated. I have conducted scientific research to prove this point, I asked a very average looking 21-year-old to like the photos of ten birds of his own age, all a seven or higher as agreed on by our panel of experts. We then asked a very unremarkable 31-year-old to give the thumbs up to a similar sample population, the results were pretty conclusive. The older guy got four times as many matches as the 21-year-old, we could partially smell the want through the app.

There is no part of the wedding day designed with the groom in mind. First there's the proposal – unless he did it in New York, Paris or parted the Shannon for it, he might as well not have bothered.

Then there's the build up, for the next few months his life is a series of tests, if he tries too hard to help he's always wrong, if he leaves her to it he's a lazy bollix.

It's all about her in the church. The photos afterwards are most normal lad's worst nightmare. At the reception he has to give a speech and has to sit through a potentially character assassination from his Best Man in his speech. With the growth of social media, most speeches don't count unless they go viral on Facebook, no pressure lads.

Then there's the dreaded first dance, seriously is this supposed to be the best day of your life or a form of punishment?

Being single isn't all doom and gloom for women either, for those who look after themselves, the benefit is that you'll end up going out with better looking more rounded individuals whose life experience will make him a more solid partner and a better long-term investment.

Wedded Bliss

Despite my very strong views on relationships and especially marriage, I always looking forward to attending my good friends' weddings. I guess it says a great deal about my character, that I can completely disregard my own feelings to share this special day in their lives, even though I'm as against matrimony as Donegal people are against safe driving.

I'm definitely a glass is half-full type of guy, so I look at the positive in every situation, a wedding is a fantastic place to score. A wedding ceremony is always an emotional melting pot. Looking up at the beautiful bride on the altar, sets off a chain reaction in the minds of single ladies: "Will it ever be me? Why am I still single? What's wrong with me?". At this point, they begin to scan the church to assess the male talent. While this is the first concerted effort to assess the male talent on show, my research has been completed weeks ago. The groom is always an invaluable source of information as to the guest list, their relationship status and the seating arrangement.

Don't worry about going to wedding alone, when all my relatives start asking why I'm still single, I tell them it's because I love one-night stands and describe my most recent conquest in detail. Strangely enough the queries regarding my relationship status have really dried up lately.

I generally find myself sitting at the singles table, which is a wonderful opportunity if you are properly prepared. I always have a few good stories about the bride and groom to regale. I take control of the betting to establish myself as the alpha male at the table. The last few weddings that I've attended, a little book has gone around to write a note to the happy couple, given my obvious writing skills this is yet another opportunity to flourish. I either use a quote from the *Notebook of Love* or some other soppy twitter account. I always write my brilliant message first, as the book is passed around the table and the competition flounders, I look like the most caring sensitive guy ever. As I lap up the admiration, all I have to do is sit back and decide which lucky lady I'll be making a coffee table out of later.

After dinner, I knock back a couple of red bulls and hit the dance floor, initially grannies, aunties and kids are the way to go. It shows you have strong social skills, have a fun side and it's a handy way of getting introduced to the single birds at the wedding, as their doting relatives are only too happy to set them up with such a charming young man.

As the night wears on – it's time to mingle, it can be very difficult to pull your moves in front of the prying eyes of your family so you need to get her out of the main room; a quick recon of the hotel before the meal begins, will provide plenty of ideal locations for a private discussion. The dynamics of your conversation can change dramatically at a wedding – you can actually discuss relationships. She will open up to you if you do it right, but instead of just nodding and agreeing, you can tell her your story of woe, be it real or imaginary, to show your sensitive side. Before the DJ has got to disc two on the best wedding album ever, you will have her upstairs in your room and she'll have something borrowed deep inside her.

Long Distance Relationships

When it comes to trends in dating, I'm better than any Ipsos MRBI poll, the sample population I assess may be slightly biased, attractive single-ish females. Nevertheless, I've got my finger on the pulse of the nation's dating habits, and anywhere else they are permitted to meander. One trend which has grown, mainly due to economic necessity rather than any seismic shift in the romantic psyche, has been long distance relationships. Countless couples have been separated due to the recession but endeavour to battle on.

As someone with an undiagnosed form of dating ADHD, these couples both impress and baffle me. Like supporters of Carlow GAA and fans of the *Twilight* movies I'll never understand it, but whatever you're into! In a rare moment of personal insight, I have to admit I attempted a long distance relationship in the recent past. I met a girl of such extraordinary beauty and charm that I barely cheated on her and at one stage considered uttering the 'G' word to her. One of the main reasons this relationship was doomed to failure, apart from a chronic inability on my behalf to commit to anything longer than a mobile phone contract, was the distance.

Despite my hectic social schedule initially, I always found time to make the arduous trek, after all, the rewards upon arrival were more than compensatory. I accept that if I was of a different mental predisposition, I may have given the relationship more effort. Like a Clare footballer when you know there's no chance of landing the ultimate prize, deep down your drive has to diminish.

When it comes to long distance relationships there are two schools of thought. One school says it's good, whilst the other says it's bad. If that's a bit complicated for you – hang on let me explain. A mate of mine refuses to date a girl living nearby, because he'd see her too much and they'd eventually break up sooner that way. He claims that seeing her at the weekend is more than enough. You can have a perfectly successful relationship this way, as he believes that they fight less because their time together is more precious. The anticipation of meeting up suspends the inevitable taking her for granted stage, prolonging the honeymoon period. As he always tells me "absence makes the heart grow fonder" but realistically what she doesn't know won't hurt him!

On the other hand, having your other half living in close proximity can have it's advantages too. You can meet up for spontaneous mid-week dates, ideal if there's no football on TV. Regular liaisons also free up the valuable weekend window, she can't complain if you want to go out with the lads, or if you have to stay in on a Saturday night because you have a massive Junior B challenge game the next morning, when you've met up a few times during the week.

If people are going to commit to a long distance relationship, I guess the key is communication. Thanks to modern technology, it's never been easier to stay in touch; whether you want to or not. Despite being half a planet apart, you guys can still get an excruciatingly detailed account of her day, the adventures of her boring friends and colleagues accompanied by smiley, winky and sad faces, monkey and thumbs down emojis to add texture to the verbal portrait she's creating.

While this is (apparently) an important and valuable element of a solid relationship, humans have an undeniable need for physical contact. Most people I know aren't yet mature enough to realise that an open relationship is the secret ingredient to a successful long distance romance. One-night stands can be every bit as important as romantic gestures to keep things fresh. Once the sex is non-emotional lads, you're doing your missus a massive favour, I'm not sure she'd see it like that so we'll keep this one to ourselves.

As for my long distance lover, like the Scottish Premier League, it used to have some attraction but that's long gone now. Who knows what the future holds? Maybe I'll change my perspective and slide the distance bar further than ten kilometres on Tinder or maybe my ex will move into the city from Loughrea and we can try again.

Sign Reading

A common question that guys ask me is how do you know if a girl is into you? Most men I know are as bad at reading the signs from women as women are at getting ready for a night out quickly. It's vital to be able to read her body language to see whether you're wasting your time with a bird that finds you as appealing as bumping into a guy's hotter ex. A few of my mates would need all women to carry round red lights like a game of *Take Me Out*, to know if they have any hope or not. There are a number of ways to tell if she's interested, for me it's if she's met me; or never heard of me.

One of the most obvious ones and a sign that I love teasing girls about is playing with her hair. Some girls do it out of habit, but more often that not in the company of someone they are attracted to, women will fiddle with their hair. I love pointing this out to a girl on a date, slagging her and telling her that it is a giveaway – she wants me so I can just relax now and enjoy myself. Each time after that when she would grab a lock, I would escalate the comments, telling her that I'm starting to worry she's falling in love, etc. It's great fun and shows you are confident, in control of the situation and all the while you are planting subliminal sexual images in her mind.

If a girl licks her lips while you are facing each other she is basically saying "kiss me" unless she's a muck savage and she's either after necking a pint of stout or devouring a well-done steak in a scene reminiscent to a scene from a wildlife documentary. Sometimes we see what we want to see and like women's infuriating selective hearing, we only gather the information we are happy to have. Reapplying lipstick (particularly red lippy) is another positive indication. If she gets some on her teeth be a gent and offer to clean it off ... with your tongue.

Body language is shockingly under appreciated as a genuine indicator of interest, especially given the fact that so much of communication is non-verbal. It doesn't take a genius to figure out that if her arms are folded and legs crossed you're about as welcome as a fart in a spacesuit. Mirroring is one of the biggest giveaways when it comes to knowing whether someone likes you or not. Take note the next time you're chatting up a girl, if you lean in does she lean in? if you sit back does she sit back? if you're both in bed together naked and you kiss her does she kiss back? Believe it or not if the answer is yes – she may like you.

Being funny is one of my many gifts, it's as good a knicker dropper as a bottle of wine. Use sexual language and in particular innuendo to steer the conversation in the direction that you want. If she appreciates and joins in, you're on to a winner, if she's taken aback or visibly upset by your comments retreat and later drop a more subtle comment to see the reaction. If she can't tolerate hearing the work dick, it's highly unlikely she's going to want to see one on the first night!

The so called experts will tell you to watch out for a flaring of the nostrils or the pupils dilating, if you actually notice any of these the poor girl is obviously as flat as the midlands and you might want to move on. The best ways to know if a girl is interested in you are, if you're an intercounty GAA player, an Interprovencial rugby player, a professional soccer player or a lottery winner then she's definitely into you.

Top 10 Turn Offs

My mother always told me not to judge a book by the cover – and how right she was. The more I frequent the bars and clubs of Galway the more I realise that the old feet to face scan simply isn't enough to properly assess the quality of a specific bird. One of the great frustrations of being a player is approaching an 8 or 9 only to find out she's seriously flawed. I've decided to compile a top ten of my own turn offs:

10 – Annoying accent

She has the face of an angel the body of a porn star. You move in with a killer line and the next thing she replies sounding like the guy from the Speakeasy ad. Ireland has a very diverse range of accents with some having the ability to create a stir down south, however some are harder to listen to than a Justin Bieber album. Specifically Cavan, Tallaght, Connemara, the Midlands, Cork and Waterford, these accents are the aural equivalent of granny knickers.

9 – Drinking Pints

I've said it before and I'll say it again, pints are for men and American tourists only. If I want to go out for pints it's with the lads not some bird I intend to be with. It shows a lack of pride in her own appearance and will lead to gaining weight. I prefer vodka drinkers or even easier again – wine drinkers.

8 – Brings up her Ex

If I'm chatting to a bird and we're getting on well and having a good time and an interesting conversation (it always is with me), there is no excuse for bringing up ex boyfriends. She should be so engrossed in the moment that thoughts of all other men are redundant, unless she's been hurt recently in which case you're more likely to end up back in her room facilitating an impromptu counselling session instead of getting to release your baby gravy.

7 – No Sense of Humour

One of the most powerful tools in the seduction game is the ability to make a woman laugh. Fortunately, I am quite witty and regularly have my targets bent over laughing before I have them bent over for another reason later in the night. I once dated a girl who didn't laugh once all night just repeated the line, "That's so funny". I couldn't help but empathise with JD in a famous Scrubs episode and dump her before I found out whether her annoying habit transferred into the bedroom.

6 – Poor Dress Sense

As a gentleman I appreciate a well dressed stylish lady, it says a lot about her character. However on a nightly basis I am visually assaulted by crimes against fashion such as fat birds wearing bodycon dresses or short shorts. Leave the fitted clothes to those who are actually fit. Girls that look like a drunken giraffe on roller skates do nothing for me either, ye spend so long getting ready to go out what harm would another 20 minutes do practising how to walk like a human being.

5 – Gay Best Friend

I don't have any problem with gay men in particular, however, they are generally massive cock blocks. If I approach a babe with her female friends, I can comfortably charm them sufficiently so that they are delighted if not slightly jealous to see their friend head off with me, gay guys on the other hand, provide a much tougher obstacle and one I'm not too keen to overcome, I have prepared for every kind of negative answer from a bird and use my tried and tested techniques to great effect, there is no way I'm going to use these lines on a guy.

4 – Jealousy

If a bird gets jealous when other birds say hello to me this spells trouble. Recently this really cool chick I was banging, correctly guessed 38 out of 54 conquests on my Facebook pictures and she was cool even pointing out a few she wouldn't mind sharing with me, she – my friend – has potential. A green eyed monster can jog on, if she is getting angry because I'm getting more attention than her, imagine what she'd be like when I'm off doing the dirt on her.

3 – Won't Buy a Drink

This shows she's going to be high maintenance. I always treat my dates very well and pay for dinner and drinks, etc. However, I expect my date to at least offer to pay. This permeates other aspects of her personality and I won't date a bitch, unless she's an absolute ride.

2 – Poorly Made Up

If a bird looks like here make up was applied by a child trying to colour in her face with an orange crayon, good luck. Also if there is evidence of facial hair waxing, I'll give that a miss, nobody wants to be kissing Freddie Mercury or Tom Selleck, since women always let themselves go in relationships this problem can become a major issue. Fake tan is also as much a part of a woman's outfit on a night out as shoes or a dress – please, please, learn how to apply it properly.

1 – Won't Put Out on the First Night

If you're looking for a relationship that's fine but it'll be very clear from the outset that I'm just looking for one thing. Birds that waste VTR (Valuable Riding Time) are one of the biggest blights on the dating scene. Sex is built up far too much, it's just a bit of fun and should be the natural end to a night out on the town.

Signing Off

L ike Dostoyevsky, Ernest Hemingway and Beethoven, I too have suffered for my art. One of the unfortunate results of being a dating guru is having to listen to women that you're never actually going to sleep with, but whose insights give me a greater understanding of the inane and incoherent mentality of the fairer sex. One concrete conclusion that I have come to, is that the ideal partner is what's commonly known as a chauvinist. Like telling a bird that her make-up looks like it was applied with a machine gun – women don't want to hear it, but it's best they know the truth.

For some reason people have suddenly got a problem with the age old *status quo*, political correctness gone mad if you ask me. Our ancestors were able to accept their roles that were determined by our physical design, the men were hunter-gatherers and the women nurtured the homestead. We were created to work in harmony like vodka and red bull, individually efficient but combined, accomplish far more. While society has evolved, us men no longer need to slay a sabre-toothed tiger to feed the family and women take their rightful position in the workplace. I believe there's still a place for old-fashioned values when it comes to romance and relationships.

I can smell the burning bras as feminist take arms against my sensible sentiments, but hear me out ladies – there are innumerate advantages to dating a man of my mental disposition. A gent sharing my ideals will take control of the situation, he won't expect the bird to do the chasing, he pays for dinner, he selects when and where you go out, he acts like a man. Sure he's checking out your ass when he opens the door for you, but take it as a compliment. After all chivalry is merely a byproduct of chauvinism.

Remember girls, while you complain about us being bastards, it's because that's exactly what you want – trust me.

We men need to embrace our masculinity, because despite what certain groups of women tell us, women still want a manly man. There's nothing wrong with an interest in fashion and a bit of grooming, but all within reason. Popular sexual fantasies back up these assertions, women use daydreams to drool over the likes of, firemen, pilots, police officers and business men in suits, not hairdressers, wedding planners or air hosts. A quick look at the best-selling outfits for the ladies in Ann Summers include the Naughty Nurse, Sexy Secretary and a PVC French Maid. It really doesn't take a genius to work out how our minds work and what people really want. Do I even need to mention a certain best selling trilogy due to hit the big screens soon?

Man up lads, you don't need to be a billionaire to satisfy her inner Goddess.

Before I bid you farewell I'll leave you with my top five tips ...

1 – *Love Yourself*

Not like that, but the way some guys approach dating, it's the only love they'll get. If you're comfortable in your own skin this is very clear to those you interact with. Who would you prefer to hang out with, some miserable craic vacuum or the guy who is up for a laugh and has a positive outlook on life? Having a full active life is the key here, hobbies and interests that get you out meeting people. My very scientific research has found that many women find a high self-esteem almost as attractive as a large bank balance.

2 – *Be Interested*

This can be difficult because there are so many boring self-absorbed people out there. Humans are receptive beings, so when you show interest it will be reciprocated. Have backup topics to discuss in case of a conversation lull, my tip is to discuss her TITS, (Travel, Interests, Television, Shopping) something she'll enjoy talking about. Women want a man that's genuinely interested in what they have to say, if you can fake this you'll never be stuck for a date.

3 – *Get Connected*

Online dating is where it's all at now. From Tinder to Meet2Cheat and everything in between, it's never been as easy to meet the love of your life from the comfort of your own couch. A good profile picture is essential and a decent bio, for a nation of talkers it's amazing how we get stuck for a few words when faced with any kind of application form. Telling the truth isn't essential online, but remember you're hoping to meet this bird you've told that you have an athletic build, if the only sport you're in shape for is Darts you certainly won't get to see her double tops later.

4 – Keep Your Options Open

Call me an old romantic, but I am searching for the perfect woman, I've met most of the wrong ones so far, but in true romcom fashion, I'll never give up on my dream. In a practical sense this means meeting as many women as possible. Mistakenly many guys when dating, clear the roster to focus exclusively on this girl. Big mistake – it's ruining your chances of meeting *the one*. The trick is to date as many as possible, comparing girls with others that you're actively dating, gives you a better perspective of each girl's pros and cons. A huge blunder many guys make initially is smothering a girl with attention – you need to make her want you. By dating numerous girls, you're not over-thinking things with any one girl, thus allowing the relationship that has the best chance of success to flourish naturally. How proud would any girl be to know you picked her ahead of four other girls you were dating at the same time?

5 – Ask Her Out

It sounds simple but is still pretty rare. Most Irish relationships begin in nightclubs, if you hook up three or four weeks in a row you're going out. Unrequited love is one of the worst feelings imaginable, imagine how many great couples there could have been if both parties knew how the other felt. Guys need to grow a pair. The answer won't always be yes, even I have faced rejection in the past, but I don't let it get me down. Sure I get blown off, but I also get blown a lot.